Tina Bruce

Cultivating Creativity

For babies, toddlers and young children
2nd edition

HODDER
EDUCATION
AN HACHETTE UK COMPANY

Orders: please contact Bookpoint Ltd, 130 Milton Park, Abingdon, Oxon OX14 4SB.
Telephone: (44) 01235 827720. Fax: (44) 01235 400454. Lines are open from 9.00–5.00,
Monday to Saturday, with a 24-hour message answering service. You can also order through
our website: **www.hoddereducation.co.uk**

If you have any comments to make about this, or any of our other titles, please send them to
educationenquiries@hodder.co.uk

British Library Cataloguing in Publication Data
A catalogue record for this title is available from the British Library

ISBN: 978 1 4441 3718 7

First Edition Published 2004
Second Edition Published 2011

Impression number   10 9 8 7 6 5 4 3 2
Year   2014, 2013, 2012

Hachette UK's policy is to use papers that are natural, renewable and
recyclable products and made from wood grown in sustainable forests.
The logging and manufacturing processes are expected to conform to the
environmental regulations of the country of origin.

Cover photo © dpaint – Fotolia.
All photography © Andrew Callaghan
Typeset by Pantek Arts Ltd, Maidstone, Kent.
Printed in Dubai for Hodder Education, an Hachette UK Company, 338 Euston Road, London NW1 3BH.

Contents

Acknowledgements

Life has moved on since I wrote the first edition of this book, but I find that once again I am very grateful for the support of my family. I should also like to thank Camilla Curtis for her creative and lateral thinking in the use of her expert knowledge as a physiotherapist. Thank you to Elizabeth Bevan Roberts for her wise and helpful thoughts, and to Andrew Callaghan for his sensitive understanding in the photographing of young children. Thank you also to Colin Goodlad for his invaluable help, Gemma Parsons and Chloé Harmsworth at Hodder.

The author and publisher would like to thank the following for permission to reproduce material in this book:

Poem reproduced with permission from Peter Dixon from his collection of education poems entitled *Weepers: A Collection of Poems Lamenting the Disgraces of the National Curriculum in Primary and Nursery Education* (Peche Luna Publishers).

Every effort has been made to obtain necessary permission with reference to copyright material. The publisher apologises if inadvertently any sources remain unacknowledged and will be glad to make the necessary arrangements at the earliest opportunity.

Introduction

Creativity, Imagination and Play are words which have been important to me, both during my own childhood and throughout life's journey. I have always considered creativity to be at the heart of what an educated person needs to be. I thought this even before I left school. I noticed that teachers who brought out and cultivated creativity in the children they taught developed a love of learning in their pupils in a way that teachers who emphasised conformity and rule of grammar did not. Learning was pedestrian with those procedure-bound teachers. I should like to pay tribute to the teachers who encouraged creativity in my life: Joyce Greaves, Bertha Milner, Leslia Marjoribanks, Chris Athey, Sybil Levy.

I remember with pleasure how our children, Hannah and Tom, would try to fend off bedtime with the cry, 'But I can't stop doing this painting, or making this model, or building this den, or playing this story,' and so on and so forth, 'because … it's creative!' They knew I would not be able to resist.

Creativity, like play and imagination, is a deeply complex concept. It spreads beyond the narrow dimension of what happens in many schools and educational settings, and is to be found in the arts, sciences and humanities, across time and space. Creativity is a worldwide issue, which holds in it the essence of what it is to be a fulfilled and fully functioning person. It celebrates the possibilities of the human mind.

The aim is that, having read the book, practitioners and parents will be in a stronger position to cultivate creativity. We owe it to our children to continue learning about our own creativity. Education, as opposed to academic hoop jumping, feeds our hearts as well as our minds.

1 Can anyone be creative?

We often hear people say, 'I'm not creative.' Perhaps they are not. But that may be because they have never been encouraged to be creative.

Isadora Duncan, a great innovator of dance in the early twentieth century, whose creativity developed a new strand of modern dance based on natural movements such as running, jumping and skipping, wrote in her book:

> I wonder how many adults realise that by the so-called education they are giving their children, they are only driving them into the commonplace and depriving them of any chance of doing anything beautiful or original.
>
> (Duncan, 1930: 30)

This book shows how parents and practitioners who:

* live with, work with and love children;
* are committed to helping them learn deeply;
* want to do so in ways which are satisfying to the child as a learner;
* want to work with children in ways which encourage them to go on learning

can give children more than pedestrian, uninspiring, commonplace learning experiences, and help them, through their play, to become imaginative and creative learners, with a will to keep learning.

Dispelling some myths about creativity

There is much confusion about creativity. We need to dispel such confusion, because it holds back our work with children and constrains their possibilities to become creative learners.

The myth that creativity is an innate gift or talent

There is a strong tendency to believe that creativity is a gift with which only some people are born. It seems to run in families. We hear people say, 'They are a very musical family,' and it seems that each new generation is as musical as the last. Perhaps the family has developed ways of encouraging the creativity of its children, so that they are, throughout their lives, creative learners. Perhaps more families could be creative in the arts, sciences and humanities, given more help in knowing how to encourage it.

We need to overcome the myth that creativity is a gift, an innate talent, that you are born either with or without. This book will show that creativity can be an important part of every human life. We can cultivate creativity in every baby, toddler and child, and hope that it will continue into adult life. Human brains allow us to:

* move (sitting, crawling, lying down, or walking, running and jumping);
* learn though our senses and movement feedback;
* develop embodiment and a sense of self as separate from but connected to others;
* communicate in words, intonation, pauses, cadence and rhythm, gestures and body language;
* have ideas and thoughts;
* have feelings;
* develop relationships;
* play so that we are innovative, flexible and are not pinned down to one result;
* imitate by reconstructing what others do;
* make mental images (visual, auditory, olfactory, taste, tactile) and imagine;
* remember;
* represent, keeping hold of our experiences and going beyond the here and now;
* become a symbol user by making one thing stand for another;
* be creative, giving an existence to ideas, thoughts, feelings, relationships and physical embodiments.

All of these brain processes contribute to and help in the cultivation of creativity. They are each important in different ways. Creativity emerges out of the coordination of these broad-ranging processes.

The myth that only a genius can be creative

In this book we shall explore different kinds and layers of creativity. We shall focus on what it means to be a creative learner. It is very rare for someone to bring unique, completely original creativity to the world, but we can be everyday creators and, in doing that, we shall enrich our lives and our learning. We see creativity in children as they play.

Original and world-shaking creativity

We shall look at truly **original creativity**, which is rare to find, because it is an act of creativity that is unique in human history. However, because it is so unusual, we shall not make this the main focus of the book. We do need to bear in mind, though, that we may be teaching or have in our group a child who will either be encouraged or constrained by us, but who will one day become a famous creator. This amusing poem by Peter Dixon helps us to think about this!

Calling the Register

Teachers never know what might become of the faces in their classes:

> Pens down…
> I said 'pens down' Tolstoy,
> And that includes you Shakespeare…
> And you Brontë.
> Right – look this way everyone –
> Nelson, I said *this* way.
> That's better…
> And you can take that grin off your face Groucho –
> Nobody thinks you're funny.
> Right – this way everyone.
> Marconi, did you hear what I said…?
> And where do you think you're going Oates?
> And you Magellan, just sit yourselves down.
> That's better.
> Stop waving your arm Hitler!
> That's much better, much better.
> Gogh… leave your ear alone,
> And don't touch that piano Beethoven.
> OK everyone –
> See, you can be sensible when you want to be,
> Even you Da Vinci,
> And you Einstein.
> Picasso stop doodling –
> Art lesson's over,
> It's time for the poetry programme.
> Who knows how to switch the television on?
> No, not you Baird.
> Livingstone, you can do it today…
> Livingstone?
> Livingstone?
> Has anyone seen Livingstone?
> Sit down Stanley!

Recreating what was previously created, but got lost in the mists of time

There is a great deal of reinventing the wheel. The Romans invented under-floor central heating, which was reinvented at a later point in history. Creations are regularly lost in a particular culture and then found again later by someone creative, or by a creative group of people who cooperate with each other.

Specialists who create ideas which are important in their field, who may not become famous, but who contribute in important ways

In science, the humanities and the arts, we find people who are very creative and who help their field or discipline to move forward. Some will become well known and famous within or beyond their area of expertise; some will not, and won't become household names.

Everyday creativity that makes life worth living

The major emphasis of this book is on the everyday creativity which can be part of anyone's life, beginning with babies, toddlers and young children, and parents and practitioners working with them. Everyday creativity is what lifts the experience of children and adults out of being pedestrian and commonplace, and enables them to do things which are creative and imaginative. Play makes a huge contribution to the development of creativity and imagination in young children. This will give them what the psychologist Maslow (in Storr, 1989: 201) calls the ability to become 'lost in the present' because they are able to live the moment to the full. They become 'totally immersed, fascinated and absorbed in the present'. These important moments free us from other people, so that our authentic voice, our deeper self, can emerge and be strong. This is as true for children as it is for adults.

Everyday creativity brings quality to our lives. It is about creative learning and so values the processes of creativity, the developing of ideas alongside the hatching of them. Expert creators, or world-shattering creators, hatch mega-important creations. Most of us bring to fruition creations which are important for us as individuals, within our families and among those we love and are loved by. They are just as important as the world-shattering creations. For those who work with or bring up young children, the more we can learn about how to help creative learning for all, the more we help individuals and how they can contribute to the world as well as finding the fulfilment that creativity brings into their lives. Fulfilment is deeper than happiness or enjoyment – it helps us through the difficult times as well as the easier side of our lives.

The myth that creativity applies to the arts more than to the sciences or humanities

One of the most serious problems in relation to creativity is the widely held myth that creativity is a process in the human brain and culture which applies only to the arts. It is rarely discussed in the context of the sciences or the humanities.

Creativity in the sciences

Every time a scientist develops a new theory or invention, he or she has created something. The Victorians were great inventors and the Industrial Revolution produced huge changes, with a wealth of new machinery and contraptions of all kinds both at home and in the workplace. Theories are abstract things, but nevertheless they are creations.

Creativity in the humanities

The humanities are about geography, history, religious and cultural studies. The study of these areas of knowledge leads us to consider issues of equality, human rights, cultural diversity and the environment. For example, the relationship between transglobal corporations and their impact on the environment (Elkington, 2001).

Creativity in the arts

Some art forms use words and signs, but others do not. We respond emotionally to different art forms and the subjects they engage with. We are influenced in doing this by our own interests, by our family and by cultural impact.

> **Non-verbal art forms** – dance; music; visual arts – two-dimensional; visual arts – three-dimensional.
> **Verbal art forms** – drama; poetry; literature; songs.
> **Creativity in other aspects of life** – sports; cookery; economics.

The myth that performance arts and creativity are the same

People often confuse performance and creativity. In fact, they are sometimes the same but often they are quite different.

A **performer** takes what, for example, a writer, poet, dance choreographer or music composer has created and **interprets** it.

A director of a theatre, dance or music group will lead the actors, dancers or musicians into an interpretation of the creator's work. The interpretation is the fascination both for the performers and for the audience.

Shakespeare may have written the play *Romeo and Juliet*, but every interpretation is different. The film directed by Baz Luhrmann portrayed the text as gang wars between two powerful families in Los Angeles, and the drugs scene. This is not something Shakespeare would have known about but it is a valid and fascinating interpretation which works for modern audiences.

A very difficult thing for playwrights, film writers, composers and choreographers is that, unless their work is performed, their creations cannot live. This is why their area of work is called 'the **performing arts**'. Sometimes the writer may also be the performer, but not necessarily.

The place, space and time are important when a creation is performed, for example Pavarotti singing what is often now called the 'football song', or the Maori dancers at the Opening Ceremony of the Commonwealth Games in 1990.

A potter went to see a performance of a play by an amateur dramatics group, directed by her friend. Afterwards she said to her friend, 'I feel sorry for you, because once the play's season is finished, you have nothing left; but when I create a pot, it remains, unless someone breaks it.' The play director replied,

'But I have made some new friends, and had new thoughts and feelings, which mean that I will never be the same again; nor will the cast or the audience. It's a good feeling. I know myself better than I did before, and I experienced working together in a group to make something together which we could share with audiences. It is an amazing thing, and part of the fascination is the way that each audience is so different, which makes each performance different. The audience influences the way the cast perform. It's all part of the fascination of performance. I wouldn't have missed it for anything. It doesn't matter that it is here and then gone.'

We have all experienced a marvellous performance, whether it is being at a club where the DJ performs the feat of mixing with great skill to make the transition from one record to the next; hearing an orchestra perform; seeing a comedian perform; seeing an Indian dance company; or going to a concert at the O2. Some performances are moments in our lives which we carry with us for ever. They are group experiences and the audience is a crucial part of them, as are the performers who interpret the dance, music, plays, etc. that either they or others have created.

Improvisations – performers and creators in the same person

Sometimes the performers and the creators are the same people. This is so in the case of jazz or improvised dance and drama. People may have an idea that they develop spontaneously together, taking turns and tuning into each other's ideas. There may or may not be an audience watching and listening. The emphasis here is much more on participation.

In the 1960s people experimented with the boundaries between audience, creator and performer. However, members of the audience often reported that they felt frightened when plucked out of their seats and included in the play – perhaps put on trial as a suspect for Jack the Ripper!

Another example of a performer being a creator is the modern development of the role of the DJ, who improvises scratch music while playing the vinyl records chosen for the purpose.

Mixed media

During the 1960s there was also wider experimentation with mixing dance, music, drama and the visual arts. Until then, opera had been the main example of this kind of mix.

In the last few years, there has been greater development in mixing film, dance, drama, music, the visual arts and the use of installations. The performance may take place in a specific place, which cannot be changed. For example, Merce Cunningham, a pioneer choreographer of modern dance, put on performances by his dance company at the Tate Modern Gallery in the Turbine Hall, which is a vast space. The dances would work only if they were performed there. He used architecture, art, film, dance and music, all together.

The visual arts – two- and three-dimensional

Those artists who create paintings, drawings, sculptures or ceramics, or who work with fine arts and crafts, vary in the degree to which they feel the need for an audience. Their creations can exist without anyone seeing or appreciating them. Most artists, however, want to share their work with an audience. Few would say they do not care about whether or not they have an audience, and it is rare that they would argue that they create their work only for themselves. Most visual artists are delighted if people want to buy their creations, to be patrons of their art and fund them, or to see their creations in public exhibitions and galleries. Perhaps, though, it is from the world of the visual arts that the idea of the lonely artist has arisen.

The myth that creative people are unhappy, unstable, difficult temperamentally and unfulfilled

Being creative is not about retreating from unhappiness (Storr, 1989: 123). When we talk about famous creative people, we tend to conjure up visions of artists starving in attics, with their poems, paintings and sculptures unsold. We hear how music composers and dance choreographers struggle to have their work performed. We are told about scientists and inventors whose theories and inventions go unrecognised. It is certainly true that most cultures do not reward creativity with high status or remuneration.

We also hear that someone has an artistic temperament or has creative genius, so is liable to outbursts of temper, sulking or sarcasm. As we shall see later in the book, just before our most creative moments we do become physically restless and uncomfortable with ourselves, but this does not have to take the form of unkind or unacceptable behaviour. Many creative people have found ways of dealing with this part of the creative process positively and constructively. There is a great problem only if others expect creative people to be difficult to live with, and make excuses for them to behave thoughtlessly to others. Then this becomes a self-fulfilling prophecy, and creativity will be linked with difficult personalities who are unhappy with themselves.

Young people in the UK are choosing to study, in secondary schools and beyond, subjects which explore and encourage creativity, such as the creative arts. It is interesting to consider why this is so. Storr (1989: 123) believes that 'people who realise their creative potential are constantly bridging the gap between the world of external reality and the inner world of the psyche'. Being creative helps us to experience life as worth living, and to feel more fulfilled.

It may well be the case that creative people are more tuned into their own feelings, thoughts, relationships and bodies, and so are more sensitive and aware of these aspects of living. It means that they are likely to experience life very fully, and so it is important that they are helped from an early age to be courageous learners, with a sense of adventure, able to take risks, dare to make mistakes and have a go, try alternatives, rearrange what they know or try out new ways of working.

Creative people often remember their childhood vividly, including the pain, joy, humiliations, guilt, shame, unfairness, love and magical moments.

Making connections is at the heart of creativity

Competent learners are able to make connections, be imaginative and creative and to represent their experiences, ideas, feelings and relationships. All of these components are important in becoming a creative person.

Our creativity helps us to see the world in different ways, and to make new connections with what we know and feel. Far from creativity causing us to be sad, lonely, unpleasant and unfulfilled, instead it helps us to be integrated people who find our inner selves and unity with ourselves. Froebel, the pioneer educator (1782–1852), held the view that one of the most important things we do when we educate our children is to help them to see themselves in all their relationships. He meant by this that we need to know and relate to ourselves, others and the universe.

Creativity is rather like play

Play anchors children and supports them in being integrated, whole people. Play also supports creativity. This similarity between play and creativity is explored in the companion book to this one, *Learning Through Play: Babies, Toddlers and the Foundation Years, 2nd Edition* (2011). In that book, the emphasis is on the ways in which play contributes to the development of learning. In this book, the emphasis is on how creativity, when cultivated, also contributes in deep and far-reaching ways to our learning. Both creativity and play are processes in the human brain which help us to reach our highest moments of learning and understanding.

The myth that children with disabilities and learning difficulties cannot be creative

One of the most amazing things about being a human is the possibility in the brain of going beyond the here and now. Human beings can think about the past and the future, as well as the present. This releases us from the constraints of immediate survival and allows us to plan ahead; to use the past as a powerful resource; to rearrange our ideas, and later, adapt them and be creative and imaginative. Children begin to do this in their play, which helps them into creative and imaginative thinking.

Some children with complex needs and learning difficulties may not develop the possibility for thinking beyond the here and now. But this does not rule out the chance of the child being creative. Until the 1970s it was thought that a proportion of children, measured according to IQ, were incapable of being educated. This was found to be untrue. During the 1990s much progress was made in developing the play of children with complex needs and learning challenges (Nielsen, 1992; Orr, 2003; Ockelford, 2008). Play and creativity are closely linked, and can be encouraged in children with disabilities and learning difficulties by emphasising learning through the senses and movement (Bruce, 1991, 2004, 2011a, 2011b; Bruce *et al.*, 2010). This is important for all children.

However, children with emotional and behavioural difficulties are able to access full and rich free-flowing play, using their senses, movement and also engaging in imaginative and creative play, in the same way as most other children.

The myth that creativity encourages revolution, chaos and anarchy

Relationships with other people are important. There is a tendency to conform and do as others do. It is very difficult to be different. Respecting difference (ethnicity, identity, culture, disability, age, etc.) is important, and this is now embedded in the legislation of countries in many parts of the world.

But it is not only in the areas of human rights, justice and equalities that an important place needs to be given to 'difference'. It is also of central importance to creativity. Sometimes creative people disturb others. But this does not make them revolutionaries or anarchists, attempting to destroy the existing stability and order. They are simply people who make us think anew, and that can challenge us, jolting us out of our comfort zones. We might:

* be fascinated and eager to find out more;
* be angry because we have to change how we think and do things;
* try to stop them, so that we don't have to change.

In fact, one of the signs of intelligent behaviour is the ability to adapt and change, and to make new connections. Creativity is about these things. We can often live more deeply if we adjust to what some creative person, or team of people, has brought into existence.

Clearing the way for the cultivation of creativity

In this book, the term 'cultivation' is used in Vygotsky's sense. When discussing good ways of helping young children to become writers, he states that:

* children must feel the need to write;
* they must have a reason of their own for writing;
* it must all happen quite naturally.

Vygotsky says:

> Writing should be 'cultivated' rather than 'imposed'.
>
> A child approaches writing as a natural moment in her/his development, and not as training from without …
>
> the best method is one in which children do not learn to read and write but in which both these skills are found in play situations.

(Vygotsky, 1978: 118)

When we try to impose learning of any kind on children instead of cultivating its development, we are likely to put children off future learning. Young children are eager to please the adults they love and spend time with, and so they try to conform to our demands. Sometimes we do more damage than good because of this.

In this chapter we have cleared away some of the confusion that exists about creativity. We have seen that:

* Anyone can be creative
* But some people are astoundingly creative
* Some creative ideas get lost, and are found again by others at different times in history and in different parts of the world
* Performance is a means of sharing a creation with an audience
* Creative people can be found in every aspect of our lives, including the arts, sciences, humanities, sports and everyday living
* Far from being difficult and unhappy, creative people find their lives are inwardly fulfilling and satisfying
* Being creative does not make someone revolutionary and dangerous. It means they have new ideas.

The new ideas people have might be new to them, new in their culture and time of history, or new to the world. Every layer of creativity is an important contribution to human living.

Reflective questions

How creative are you? For example, do you create your own recipes when you cook, or make greetings cards of your design to give to friends and family? How do you landscape your garden and choose to arrange plants? If you don't have a garden, how do you arrange the living area?

Useful texts

It is useful to read about the lives of creative people to gain more insight into creativity and its processes. An example of good reads in this respect are:

Keynes, R. (2002) *Annie's Box: Charles Darwin, his Daughter and Human Evolution.* Fourth Estate: London.

Langer, E. (1997) *The Power of Mindful Learning.* Addison/Wesley Publishing Company: Harlow.

2   What is creativity?

Having dispelled some myths about creativity in Chapter 1, in this chapter we are going to establish what creativity is in order to begin to tease out what makes a learning environment that is conducive to the cultivation of creativity. We need to be sure that we know what it is that creative everyday living offers children and the adults who live and work with them. We need to be clear why the cultivation of creativity (closely linked with childhood play) should have a central place in encouraging the development and learning of children.

Creativity and the individual

The need for love, companionship and feeling we matter to others

Every child growing up has a need to feel that they are loved and that they matter to at least someone. Companionship that gives love, warmth and affection is part of this. Feeling we belong with others is central to developing well-being. So is being acknowledged and affirmed.

This is very different from saying that children should always be socialising and interacting with other people. We all need personal space. Otherwise we cannot develop our self-identity and be self-aware individuals. The original meaning of the word 'individual', according to Abbs (in Storr, 1989: 80), was 'indivisible and collective'. Now it means the exact opposite. 'Individual' in modern usage means being a distinct person, aware of and conscious of our separate self.

Being creative encourages us to know ourselves and gives us independence and a sense of agency. This means that we do not feel under the control of others and that we can do things ourselves.

Belonging but separate

Children and adults need both a sense of belonging and to be aware of themselves as separate, creative individuals. The neurologist Antonio Damasio (1999) believes that self-awareness is an important part of the creative process.

Children who are encouraged to develop their creativity are helped to develop a point of view of their own, which will not be overdependent on others. Research shows (Bettelheim, 1977; Storr, 1989: 81; Kitzinger, 1997) that when children do everything as a group, they develop a group identity with shared feelings. This seems to discourage creativity. This is because they are less likely to do something different from the others. Doing something different, new and original is central to creativity. Creativity is part of the process through which children begin to find out they have something unique to 'say', in words or dance, music, or hatching out their theory.

Developing our interests

Having and developing our own interests is an important part of our lives and is linked with creativity. If we always depend on other people, expect to share all our activities and daily lives with others, and depend on having close relationships with other people as the main source of satisfying lives, then we cannot be fully functioning individuals. We won't have any interests that are our own, so we won't have the possibility to develop, through our creativity, our ideas and points of view. This means we won't be able to bring into existence new ideas, do things in a new way, or make things that are different. We will always follow the crowd.

Enjoying and being able to use our personal space creatively

Winnicott (1971: 29) argues that enjoying our own company is a positive thing and a sign of emotional maturity. The journey towards this begins when babies and toddlers enjoy personal space while in the company of people they love and are comfortable with. Because they don't have to worry about things, because they feel safe and secure, they begin to explore their feelings and ideas, to make discoveries and be inventive and innovative. They can become creative. What they do might not be original, world-shaking acts of creation but it is new to them, and so it is an example of what we are going to call 'everyday creativity'.

Some of us continue to enjoy being alone in the company of friends and people who are important to us, taking our personal space and developing our deepest thoughts and creativity in that context. Others like to be alone, having learned as babies and young children to think well, with creativity and insight, during times of complete personal space.

Winnicott's (1971) theory has helped us to think about the beginnings of creativity, and Vygotsky (1978) is also very useful in this respect. He suggests that the highest forms of thinking begin in a social relationship. Here we see the baby and the adult together, but giving each other personal space in which the baby can discover how to be a creative, thinking, reflective person.

Feeling emotionally safe enough to be creative

In the last chapter we saw how important it was to dispel the myth that creativity requires a state of emotional instability or neurotic personality. Winnicott (1990) shows us that the opposite is true. In order to be creative we need to feel sufficiently emotionally safe to go on creative adventures on our own. We have to be apart from others in our minds.

We need companionship and love, and to feel that we are part of things, but we also need to have the personal space to be independent, separate, autonomous, with ideas of our own, and to be creative. We belong, yet we need to be separate from others, too.

Being a creative person brings a different kind of satisfaction to life. People who depend on the group to tell them how and what to think are not very confident about life. They are anxious about being alone, because they can't think things through or decide what to do on their own. They can't find their own way. Creative people can do this. They are good problem solvers. They like adventures with ideas. They are fascinated by the creative experience of thinking of new ideas.

A creative person's most significant moments are those which give new insight and new discovery, often alone. But daring to think for yourself and to have your own ideas requires the courage that comes from being emotionally able to do this. Early positive experiences of feeling separate but feeling connected to others are an important part of this. Vygotsky (1978) gives us the cognitive theory for why this is so. Winnicott (1971) helps us to understand the emotional reasons.

Group creativity

In cultures in which the purpose of painters, sculptors, dancers, musicians, storytellers, writers, etc. is to serve the community by giving expression to traditional wisdom, techniques are valued but not the creativity of an individual (Storr, 1989). This book is about both individual and group creativity. We have had a brief look at what is involved in individual creativity; now we will consider some of the important issues surrounding the development of group identity.

We saw in Chapter 1 that groups of people join together and share creative ideas, particularly in relation to scientific projects, drama, music and dance improvisations. This is very different from what Storr (1989) calls 'forced gregariousness', which is not a creative experience. Joanna Glover (2000), writing in her book about children composing music, agrees with Storr about the importance of not forcing gregariousness, but instead giving children opportunities for what Storr calls solitude and Glover calls 'aloneness'.

Aloneness with music is essential for the youngest children and important for most children. Children with special educational needs and disabilities/complex needs often enjoy music and appreciate the opportunity to listen quietly in their own personal space, as Adam Ockelford's work shows (Ockelford, 2008). Groups develop traditions in the way they perform which can become interpreted as required ways of working. This can constrain the creativity needed in composing. Composing alone can be seen as both a creative need and a learning process. 'It is not until a child has all the control in his or her hands, so to speak, that both aurally and kinaesthetically the feeling of making the music comes fully home. The freedom to take flight in an improvisation, unchecked by anyone else, or to find a musical idea, re-run it, transform, repeat and work over something in your own time, alone, allows a train of thought to develop and find its own shape' (Glover, 2000: 130).

This notion of being creative alone while in a community of companions is a recurrent theme in the literature on creativity. Being near people who are sensitive to our need to be alone in a crowd is helpful. Sometimes other children and adults are engaged in the same pursuits, but not always. In early childhood settings where children are encouraged to be creative learners, a first glance round the indoor areas and the garden might suggest that children are all doing different things and are not in a group at all, except when gathered by adults into organised group time for stories and singing together. A deeper look reveals that children are grouping themselves according to their interests. Where there is effective pedagogy, adults are linking the way they work with children through their direct and indirect teaching into their informed and acted-upon observations of children's learning.

Sybil Marshall, a primary headteacher and a pioneer in the teaching of creativity in the 1960s, identified the attributes of what she saw as a true educator.

A true educator:

* should know what they are trying to teach;
* should be able to help children learn;
* needs to continue with their own learning and education in order to keep broadening and deepening what they know and understand and can share with children and their families;
* understands that talking and teaching are not necessarily the same thing.
  (Marshall, 1963: 24)

She recommended (p. 120) the detailed study of one child in a group (what we now call regular observation of individual children) so that we see children as a collection of individuals rather than as fractions of a group.

The children in her village school were from 4 to 11 years of age. She gave them a group experience of listening to Beethoven's *Pastoral*; she then took them out to 'enjoy the day', which was similar to the one that inspired Beethoven to write the music. They returned to listen to the music again while taking a mid-morning snack together. This gave a shared experience out of which much creativity emerged. One of the older children, Beverley, who particularly enjoyed writing poems, said one day, after sitting without writing anything for some time, 'I simply can't write an end-of-the-day one, but there's another poem that keeps wanting to come about the symphony all together.'

Symphony

The music is slowing,
It's drawing to an end,
The rhythm is flowing
The weaving tunes still blend.
The oboes were singing,
They made a pretty air:
The violins were stringing,
The double bass was there.
The flutes, bassoons, and piccolos
In harmony agree,
And all the swelling music goes
To make the symphony.

(Beverley, in Marshall, 1963: 211)

The children in this school experienced companionship in writing, but were not expected to produce similar poems. They could develop their own ideas without pressure to conform or create. With the pressure off, they had the time to develop their ideas, incubate them, and could find moments conducive to hatching them, as Beverley did in the group-writing workshop. This is the same whether it is a mathematical idea, scientific hypothesis, dance, poem or musical composition.

This links with what Glover (2000: 131) writes about group compositions in music improvisations. The ability to find some group coherence in improvised music-making can find expression in any human group and any setting. Beyond the immediacy of improvisation, young children composing in groups often compose alone, though side by side.

Creativity brings into existence new ideas, original ways of doing things and new creations of all kinds.

Peter Hewitt, Chief Executive of the Arts Council England, says:

We must keep telling those inclined to prescription, art will never be contained, and creativity never controlled … It thrives in open spaces where it has room to breathe, where people are free to explore. It is by nature resistant to instruction or targeting. The whole point of creativity, as with all forms of innovation, is that it is impossible to know the outcome in advance.

(Hewitt, 2002: 29)

This is as true for creativity in the sciences and the humanities as in the arts.

In this chapter we have considered: what is creativity? Creativity:

* is an individual response
* requires autonomy and independence
* needs personal space
* is about feeling emotionally safe enough to create
* can be found in groups, but is not responsive to 'forced gregariousness'
* is about having new ideas and ways of doing things, and making connections.

Reflective questions

Observe a baby who can sit and/or crawl. What interests them? How long and in what ways do they concentrate on things that are of interest?

Observe a toddler and a child 3–7 years of age. Ask the same questions.

Evaluate your findings of the baby and toddler. How important is personal space in encouraging a child's concentration on what interests them? How does the child explore their interest? Do they have new ideas and ways of doing things as they explore?

Useful texts

Forbes, R. (2004) *Beginning to Play (Birth to Three Years)*. Open University Press: Maidenhead.

3 What is involved in creative learning?

Having an idea – where did it come from?

It is usually impossible to know where a creative idea came from or how it developed into a creation of some kind. This is not a conscious process. Arthur Koestler wrote a pioneering book on creativity in which he argued:

> The creative act, in so far as it depends on unconscious resources, presupposes a relaxing of the controls and a regression to modes of ideation which are indifferent to the rules of verbal logic, unperturbed by contradiction, untouched by the dogmas and taboos of so-called common sense. At the decisive stage of discovery the codes of disciplined reasoning are suspended – as they are in the dream, the reverie, the manic flight of thought, when the stream of ideation is free to drift, by its own emotional gravity, as it were, in an apparently 'lawless' fashion.
>
> (Koestler, 1964: 178)

This means that creative people:

* are not conscious of how they came to have an idea;
* have been able to relax the rules of logic they normally apply;
* have allowed themselves some 'lawless' and dream-like thinking;
* have abandoned common-sense thinking;
* have allowed their thinking to drift and meander;
* have then pulled it all together into a disciplined act of creation.

Figures 3.1–3.3 The girl is carrying hollow blocks, and is probably not aware that she is developing an idea, but is working in a dreamlike way with the blocks. As her thoughts drift and meander, she begins to pull things into shape, resulting in a fan-like creation made from the blocks.

The creative process

John Howkins (2001: 16) has developed a fivefold view of the creative process, which he calls RIDER. It is a mix of dreams and analysis:

Review: this means taking stock of things and being curious.

Incubation: creativity needs time and opportunity to form an idea, in a relaxed and unpressured way.

Dreams: drifting about in our thoughts frees us from the usual constraints of our lives.

Excitement: this gives us what Howkins (2001: 17) calls the possibilities for making 'intuitive jumps and half-calculated sideways movements'. He says that the trick is not to look before you leap!

Reality checks: we need to check that we are not straying too far in our day-dreaming, drifting and meandering thoughts. Otherwise none of the creative thinking can take shape and form.

Harris takes the view that:

> Possible or imaginable instances of magic become more widespread as children's grasp of the constraints on what is possible becomes firmer and more wide-ranging.
>
> (Harris, 2000: 166)

The creation

This seems to involve two things at once. People often report that they felt a bit like Archimedes did in his bath, or like Beverley, the ten-year-old introduced in Chapter 2 who wrote the poem to the music of Beethoven's *Pastoral*. They feel a sense of heightened awareness, full of energy and life. They are able to hold their focus very fully and very deeply. But at the same time they also feel very dreamy and their thoughts can flow in a surge of clear thinking.

It is the combination of the two and the ability of the creator to pull the two together, which takes a huge amount of energy, that allow the creation to come to fruition. People often become rather uncomfortable and tense just before the surge. Perhaps this is why creative people are seen as tense and difficult to be with. If we try to talk and interact with them just at that time, they will try to block us out, because otherwise they will quite literally lose the moment.

Jung thought that creativity involved a release of what he called 'energy-tension'. Howkins (2001: 5) says, 'He was scathing about his contemporaries' inclination to link creativity and neurosis.' He thought neurosis was an obstacle to creation.

The moment of creation has often been likened to giving birth to a baby. Because of the energy and effort of forming a creative idea which actually shapes into a creation, we tend to be very emotionally attached to what we create.

Sometimes children show no attachment to a painting or model they have made, and show no interest in whether it is put on the wall as a display or any inclination to take it home with them; at other times they do. Adults working with young children need to understand the difference between finger painting as a creative process, when ideas are probably incubating, and an act of creation. When it is a creation, the child will be likely to show interest, seeing what they have made as a product.

When working with young children, it is probably most important to put great emphasis on giving children plenty of time and space, with people sensitive to their ideas. It is therefore helpful to examine what is involved in incubation in a little more detail.

Graham Wallas (in Storr, 1989: 25) believed there is a period of **incubation** in the development of a creative idea. He suggested that this has three stages:

1. preparation;
2. simmering;
3. illumination.

After the period of incubation, a creation may be hatched out. This might be an idea or something tangible, such as a painting, drawing, sculpture, dance, song, poem, story, scientific theory, mathematical formula, social policy, recipe for a food dish, plan for a treat for a relative. Because of the huge effort and energy needed for a creative idea to take form and become a creation, most creative processes do not end with a product. We talk about the best-laid plans, which drift and meander but don't quite take form.

Children who are experiencing trauma, who are unsettled, have a low sense of well-being or are put under pressure to conform to adult-led tasks, are unlikely to be able to summon up the energy needed to think creatively and shape these thoughts into creations. This is why it is important that children are given their **right to play** (Hyder, 2004). Play is largely about creating the conditions which are conducive for creativity to develop in both process and product. While they play, children prepare, simmer and illuminate ideas, without pinning them down into creations. Unless the processes of creativity are strong, the creations will not be strong. Play supports the possibility for creative ideas and thoughts to develop. The processes of representation support children's creations.

Preparing

Creative babies, toddlers and young children will develop an interest in something and try to find out more about it. They depend on adults to create environments in which they will have enough freedom of choice to do this. They need interesting materials to explore and experiences which capture their interest. They also need adults who will help them by being informed, sensitive observers, who can tune into what it is that they are paying attention to, and who will help them to find out more.

Simmering

Rudolf Steiner (1988) believed that the period of forgetting is as important as the period of remembering. We often say we will sleep on an idea. Gopnik *et al.* (1999) say that we use what we know to make connections with what we don't know, and we need other people to help us in doing this.

In order to be creative, we need personal space and time away from forced gregariousness, to mull things over and subconsciously reflect on what has interested us. We may not even be aware that we were interested in an idea or thing.

Babies and young children depend on adults to create time both to develop interests and to let them simmer and incubate.

Illumination

This involves having an insight into how to take an idea that has been forming into creation. This is sometimes described as having insight, or as the 'a-ha!' experience. One of the most famous examples of this is the story of Archimedes in his bath. He had been gathering thoughts about volume, without fully realising it, for some time. These thoughts were simmering in his head and then, while having his bath, he had a moment of insight. The idea was then able to hatch out into what is now known as Archimedes Law:

When an object is submerged in a fluid, the upward force which this creates on the object is equal to the weight of the fluid which the object has displaced.

Corollary:

If this force is greater than the weight of the object itself, then the object will float. If it is less than the weight of the object, then it sinks.

Hatching

John Howkins (2001: 127) says there are 'commencement' incidents which start an idea going. We don't usually have any awareness that this is happening to us. This occurs during the period of preparation in the incubation process in creating an idea that comes to fruition. Of course, not all creative ideas become creations; they may stay in our heads and lead to other ideas. Some creative ideas might lead us into other creative thoughts; others emerge from deep inside us and become externalised into creations.

There is the famous example of the creative scientist who went for a walk in the countryside and saw some teasels growing on the riverbank. He thought no more about it. Somehow this memory became used in hatching out the creation of Velcro™, which on one side has teasel-like hooks and on the other side is like animal fur, easy for the hooks to attach themselves to. It has transformed the way we join material together, just as buttons and zips did when they were invented as improvements on tying with ribbon or lacing.

The gap between the commencement incident during the period of incubation and the hatching out of a creation varies. It could be hours and days, or it could be weeks and years. When we offer children experiences they find interesting, we never know where it might lead, later coming to fruition as a creation.

In his book *Mind Storms*, Seymour Papert (1980), who developed ideas important in helping people, and especially children, to use computers, remembers back to his childhood. From an early age he loved cogs. His parents noticed this interest in cogs and encouraged it. When he later created the 'Turtle' computer, which moved about when instructed by children, he made the cover transparent so that they could see the cogs he loved so much inside it.

We can see the creative process leading to a creation here. Papert had plenty of opportunity to gather experiences and ideas about cogs, encouraged by his parents to do so as a very young child. The idea of using cogs and how they move together became intertwined with his work as an adult and was used in developing machinery. He had all the time needed for this to come together in a powerful mixture and simmer.

His thoughts did come together and connect, so that he gained insight and was able to go the next step and develop his now-formed idea and hatch it out into an early form of computer, suitable for use by children and beginners.

We shall see more examples, from the arts, sciences and humanities, in later chapters.

Heightened awareness – intense feelings – feeling alive

There is often a heightened awareness as we hatch out an idea. It is a feeling of intensity, very focused and alert. It is a good feeling, although it is often followed by exhaustion and the need to relax. The hatching process must not be interrupted or it will vanish. When moments like this are interrupted, it leaves the person feeling that something has been snatched away, and it is very dispiriting. There is a feeling of loss. After all, as Winnicott (1971: 79) says, creativity 'belongs to being alive'.

In the photographs of the girl making a creation out of the hollow blocks, we saw her prepare in her mind some ideas about block construction, and that these simmered as she meandered in her dream-like state. The ideas became illuminated and came into focus as she hatched them and the ideas turned into a creation. The feelings that accompany this, of 'being alive', are part of leading a fulfilled life.

The role of the adult in cultivating creativity

Adults play a critical part in whether or not children become creative people. Unless they work sensitively with children and their families, the emergent possibilities for creativity that are in every child do not develop or can be quickly extinguished.

Adults who tune into what interests the child and who are informed participant observers are able to appreciate and value the beginnings of creativity in children without invading the child's creative idea or taking it over. They support children as they develop their autonomy and value them as individuals. At the same time, they make sure the children feel a sense of belonging.

It is helpful to look at some practical examples of adults working with children, to see what this looks like in reality.

Figure 3.4 Two practitioners are supporting the children in their block play. They are tuning into the children's ideas and actively facilitating the play, but they are careful not to invade or take over.

Being there for children – adults as anchors, who make children feel secure enough to let their creative ideas begin to flow

Often, when children arrive in the morning, they need to be near or with an adult they trust and know, with whom they have developed a warm and affectionate relationship. Sensitive companionship, as we saw in earlier sections, cultivates creativity.

Adults can arrange to be an anchor, to sit in one area and 'be there' for children in the spirit of companionship.

Being near – adults having eyes at the back of their heads, observing and aware, but respecting the children's personal space and joining in only when needed

The adult needs to be nearby, sensitive to the children and their needs.

A group of children (three and four years old) were playing with exuberance and were very lively, but well organised among themselves. They took turns, waited for each other to jump, keeping an eye to make sure that the wooden blocks they were playing with were carefully arranged. Interestingly, this creative play did not develop. They left after about five minutes.

On another day, there was an imaginary swimming pool, with children jumping into the deep end and other children pretending to be lifeguards. Somehow the mood and chemistry weren't right and the children abandoned the play. This often happens with a creative idea. For every creative idea, many fall by the wayside. Only a few ideas get through.

Figure 3.5   The toddler is being encouraged to mix powdered paint colours.

Figure 3.6   Pausing for thought.

Figures 3.7–3.8 The practitioner helps the toddler to learn how to squeeze the paint out of the container. She shows him how to do this and encourages him to persevere.

Adults guiding the children in order that a creative idea can break through and continue

We frequently find that children become frustrated, get stuck, are about to give up because they hit a problem as they play. We need to remember that, in many respects, free-flow play and developing creative ideas are the same. Neither can be pinned down. Both are about children using their experience to learn more. In free-flow play a creative idea is developed but is in a state of flow. Sometimes these ideas are pinned down and become acts of creation, either then or later. However, this is not always the case.

Returning to some of the significant aspects relating to the development of creativity discussed earlier in the chapter, we can see that there is a delicate balance here between helping the child and making the child feel a sense of agency and seeing themselves as a separate and independent individual.

Toddlers can be very rejecting of help because they want to be independent, but they can't manage to do what they want to do. This is where adults need to be particularly understanding and sensitive to the child's feelings. By holding a piece of wood still or cutting a tough piece of string but letting the child participate, constantly checking that this is what the child has in mind, the adult can support a child through a tricky moment in the creative process. Then the moment is not lost, the child has a positive experience and learns that with perseverance an idea can be developed.

Two girls (four-year-olds) are using the hollow wooden blocks but are having difficulty getting the planks to straddle the two sides. They need two planks to cover the distance, but they don't know how to prop them up, or perhaps they don't realise how to prop them up. The adult sees the problem out of the corner of her eye and joins the play. She brings the conversation round to the identification of the problem. As a consequence of the adult doing this, one of the children suggests propping the planks up with a cylinder from the wooden unit block set from the shelf behind. With the problem solved, the children are able to develop their free-flow play which contains in it their creative ideas.

Figure 3.9 Water falls off the table edge and cascades onto the floor.

Figure 3.10 The toddler is looking at the water on the floor.

Figure 3.11 The practitioner takes her hand so that she does not slip, but allows her to lead.

Figure 3.12 The practitioner senses that she will be able to balance and lets go of her hand. She does a little dance of joy, feeling her independence, yet secure with the adult near.

Helping children to know how to use materials

Every material is different and has its own characteristics. We can't expect children to know about paint or clay or dance, and what is involved in engaging with these areas, unless we help them.

Children need to be supported by adults as they learn to use materials. Clay, paint and dance (which uses their own body as the material) are three examples of the kind of help children need if their creativity is to be cultivated.

* **Clay**: The children have been helping to build a wall in the outside area. This is reflected in the way the clay is provided in that area. By showing an interest and watching what the children are doing, talking to them and listening carefully to the children's ideas, the adult can give the appropriate support to each child. One child might be interested in cutting the clay but the problem is, how do you cut a rolling ball? Another might be making small lumps of clay and putting them on the brick in a row. Children notice what other children do and they pick up on and take forward ideas which attract them. We say that imitation is a great form of flattery. Children in group settings learn as much from each other as they do from the adults. The child making the row of bricks likes the idea of spheres and puts a clay ball on the top of each brick in the row.

* **Paint**: With the help of an adult, children make, for example, finger-paint mixtures. There needs to be plenty of discussion between adult and children about what is needed. It is important to remember that a discussion is a two-way thing – it is not the adult instructing and asking questions that the child is expected to answer as a kind of test. A discussion is when people genuinely interact with each other to make a dialogue together. Doing this helps children to become more aware of their creative ideas, so that they are more likely to turn them into creations. However, finger painting is not about making lasting creations – it is all process. It is about getting to know how paint behaves, and making shapes, patterns and images which are fleeting. It gives children opportunities to gather ideas for future use. This is a huge part of creativity.

Figure 3.13 The adult talks with the children about finger painting. The girl suggests that the white paint is 'sugar'. The adult replies, 'Yes, it does look like sugar. The paint does look just like sugar.'

Gathering ideas – incubating ideas – hatching ideas

Every time a creative idea is hatched, we need to remember that it rests on an edifice of ideas gathered, built on, rearranged and altered, through a period of incubation. Not all ideas will develop to the point of becoming creations. Creativity is hugely about process and only sometimes carries through into a product.

As children become involved in using clay and finger painting they are gathering and incubating creative ideas. It is not often, with young children, that the ideas are turned into lasting creations. The emphasis is on process more than product.

Figure 3.14   The boys wrap themselves up and coordinate their movements.

Figure 3.15   Then they experiment with being upright and on the floor. They have varied their coordination from a vertical to a horizontal plane.

Figure 3.16   They are able to make a traditional wheelbarrow movement and are delighted with their technical prowess.

❋ **Dancing**: Just as the children needed support and help with the clay and the finger painting, so they need help with dancing. They can make a start by selecting their dancing clothes. Wearing dressing-up clothes often leads into dance or role-play. It helps us all to switch into the mood required for these areas of learning. For example, following the local dance school performance attended by some of the children, there is a ballet craze in the setting, and staff have supported this interest by introducing appropriate clothes, music, pictures and books. They also provide dance clothes and books about dance in a range of cultures. Once they are in their costumes, the girls want some ballet music to be played. The adult discusses with them what music they would like and, as soon as it begins, they move into attempts at arabesques, toe pointing and second-position arm movements. This is creative in the sense that, although they are using ideas they have gathered about dance, they are putting them together in their own way. As so often happens, they are watched with interest by another child, in this case the child on the rocking horse, who may or may not have seen ballet. Observing what other children do is a major way in which children gather ideas which they later use creatively.

The child as a separate individual needing personal space and also feeling connected to others through a sense of belonging

Some people love to be alone in a crowd. A child might have an idea that does not need the support of others. However, this is possible only if the child is settled and at ease in the group setting. Unsettled children cannot develop their creativity. These are the children who worry us because they flit restlessly. Exploring different materials and moving from one to the other when you have an idea in mind which you carry with you is not flitting (Athey, 1990) – this has a focus which is missing from flitters.

Adults who are good observers of children can see the difference between a focused child developing a creative idea and needing to meander amongst materials and try things out in the service of a thought, gathering form, incubating and simmering, and a child who surges about without stopping to look at all.

Figure 3.17 The boy is introduced to roller painting.

Figure 3.18 He explores the roller.

Figure 3.19 He uses the roller on his head.

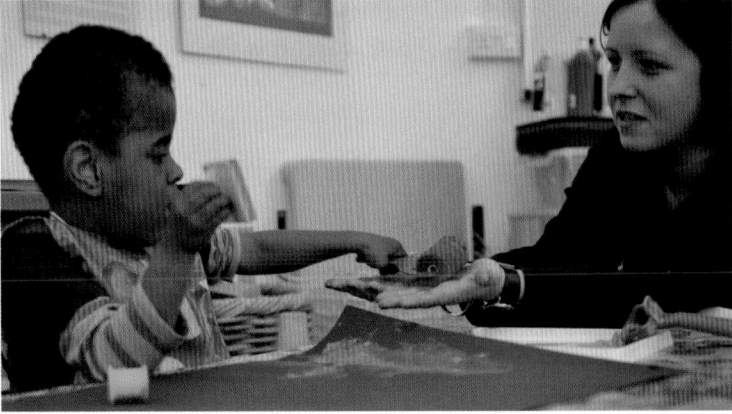

Figure 3.20 He uses the roller on his key person's hand.

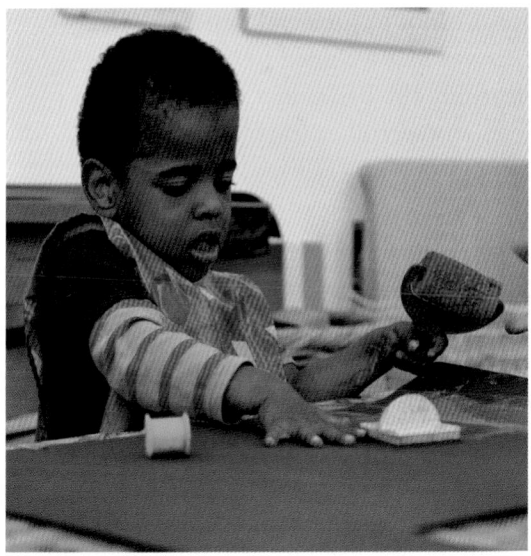

Figure 3.21 He tries to make a hand print.

Figure 3.22 His key person suggests he needs to roll some paint on his hand.

Figure 3.23 He presses with two hands to make a mark on the paper.

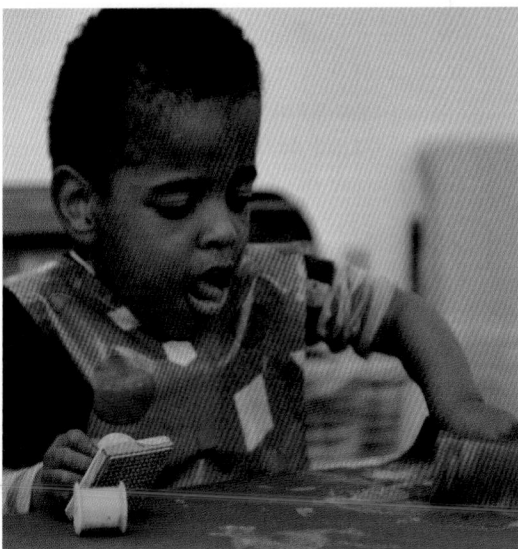

Figure 3.24 He uses the roller on the paper in the conventional way. He has used the roller to paint in a variety of ways, which are all part of the creative process.

In this chapter we have seen how important it is not to give children commonplace experiences. Ellen Langer believes that we need to develop 'mindfulness' in children. She argues that 'learning the basics in a rote, unthinking manner almost ensures mediocrity'. She gives a powerful example:

> At tennis camp I was taught exactly how to hold my racket and toss the ball when serving. We were all taught the same way. When I later watched the US Open, I noticed that none of the top players served the way I was taught, and, more important, each of them served slightly differently … Even if we are fortunate enough to be shown how to do something by a true expert, mindless practice keeps the activity from becoming our own … If we learn the basics but do not over-learn them, we can vary them as we change or as the situation changes.
>
> (Langer, 1997: 14)

Varying what we know is at the heart of creativity. We need to help our children to dare to be creative, like the girls varying what they knew of ballet to make their own dances. Varying what we know means daring to be different. That is also at the heart of creativity. If we focus on the basics and teach them in a 'one size fits all' method, we constrain children's possibilities to become creative. We have seen that this will lead to half-lived lives, which are not inwardly satisfying. Instead, we want children to have the energy, focus, diverse ideas, flexible flowing thoughts and deep satisfaction in their learning that bring them alive in the fullest sense of living. Creative learning means living to the full.

In this chapter, we have looked at:

* where creative ideas come from
* how adults can cultivate creativity
* adults as anchors
* adults who are near and 'on hand' to help
* adults knowing when to guide and give direct help
* adults helping children to gather ideas, incubate and hatch them.

Reflective questions

Consider your role as an adult in cultivating the creativity of the children you spend time with.

Look at the examples in this chapter. How do you organise materials, places and spaces? What kinds of conversations do you have with children that cultivate their creativity? How do you help children to hatch their creative ideas?

Useful texts

Bruce, T., Meggitt, C. and Grenier, J. (2010) *Child Care and Education, 5th Edition*. Hodder Education: London.

Craft, A. (2002) *Creativity and Early Years Education: A Lifewide Foundation*. Continuum: London & New York.

Duffy, B. (2009) *Supporting Creativity and Imagination in the Early Years, 2nd Edition*. Open University Press: Maidenhead, Philadelphia.

Liebschner, J. (1992) *A Child's Work: Freedom and Guidance in Froebel's Educational Theory and Practice*. Lutterworth: Cambridge.

4 Creating an environment that cultivates creativity

We know that people who love and help children to develop and learn are the most important thing in their lives. If children are to develop their creativity, they certainly need adults who cultivate this side of their learning. We need to remember that part of the adult's role is to create both an atmosphere and an environment that cultivates creativity.

In this chapter, we shall explore how we can set up the indoor area with creativity in mind. The environment plays a central part in cultivating creativity. But if organised inflexibly, it can constrain or even extinguish it.

We can do so much to encourage creativity in children and in ourselves if we think carefully:

* about the materials we offer as experiences;
* about the way we offer the material provision.

We know that the physical, direct experiences children have are fundamental to their learning about a sense of self through embodiment and connectedness to others; and we also know that these are the bases of symbolic behaviour and creativity of all kinds.

The way that we help children to interact with the material and experiences we provide will have a great impact on whether or not they develop into creative people.

Sensitive interaction on the part of adults, together with a carefully thought-through provision of the physical environment, is the key to the cultivation of creativity.

Before the children arrive

The material, physical environment needs children in it to make it come alive, and so there is always a feeling of uncanny quietness and anticipation of things about to happen when setting up the learning environment. It's a bit like a stage set before a rehearsal or a dance studio before the dancers arrive. Nevertheless, it is useful for us as practitioners to take a good look at how carefully we are thinking through our provision for children. They will not get much out of their time in a group setting if this is not an intrinsic part of the way the staff work together.

Creative entrance areas

The first thing the children will see will be the entrance area. This is where children are greeted each day by a member of staff. In cramped buildings, every bit of space is creatively put to use by the staff and children. Buildings are often full of nooks and crannies, which are very appealing to children. Books help children to reflect on their experiences and to make new connections about them. The book area should be warm, light and cosy. As well as a book corner, there should be books to support the children's experiences in other areas.

Figures 4.1–4.2 The children have made fruit salad on a number of occasions, and this story is about carrying a basket of fruit on the head – but it makes creative new connections which are greatly enjoyed by children. Stories encourage children to make new connections and rearrange their experiences in the telling of a good tale. Children often use a combination of their own real experiences and the stories they know when they make up their own stories. It is as if first-hand experience and stories they love give them a good start in their own story making.

Creative use of rooms

The children arrive each day, hopefully with the expectation that there will be interesting things on offer and knowing that there will be things specially for them as individuals. Because observation is at the heart of the teaching and informs it, the staff need to use their observations of children at play to help them plan both for the group and for individual children's learning (Bartholomew and Bruce, 1993).

When considering creative development and learning, the important things are:

* to get the indoor and outdoor environments organised so that they support the cultivation of creativity;
* that adults understand and are informed about how to help creativity to develop.

Wherever the children go, everything needs to be carefully laid out and presented. The environment sends signals to the children about how they might use it. The children need to have free access to the outdoor area (in the rain and snow with appropriate clothing for staff and children) and when the weather is warmer, they may go to the garden for their story, poetry, singing and dancing. Each child has a key person with whom they go for group times, but they will be free to use the whole of the indoor and outdoor areas throughout the rest of the session. This is what might be called a 'yes' environment – it beckons to be used.

Presentation of materials
* Displayed at child height
* Clear categories and sorted carefully
* A designated area of the room where the materials can be used nearby
* Labels with pictures and words

Wooden unit blocks

Wooden unit blocks can be presented in several ways. This might be in wheeled storage containers which can be taken into different areas. In most settings they are set out on storage shelves (book shelves). The drawings of the unit blocks, with labels on them, show the children what is there.

The wooden unit blocks all relate to each other mathematically. In this book, unit blocks are recommended for this reason: if we are going to go to the expense of a set of wooden blocks, we want to buy a set which offers the maximum possibilities. There are also hollow blocks and mini-blocks.

The wooden unit blocks are the modern form of Froebel's Gifts. Froebel (1782–1852) was an educational pioneer. He was a mathematician, scientist and forester by training. He realised the importance of play in a child's learning and designed a set of wooden blocks which he called the Gifts, which opened up possibilities for children to learn about mathematics, the arts and to develop their creativity and imagination through their play with them. Modern-day plastic blocks are rarely satisfactory because they are so difficult to balance. They are too flimsy and light, and easy to knock over. The wooden blocks should be made from wood grown in sustainable forests. A set of wooden blocks, preferably unpainted so that the grain of the wood can be experienced, is probably one of the most important materials we offer children in group settings.

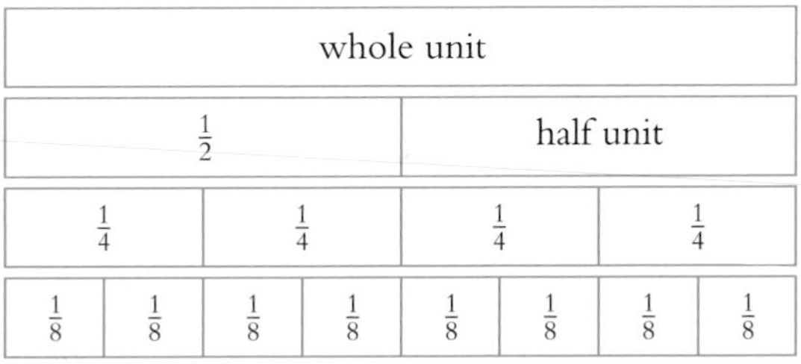

whole unit							
$\frac{1}{2}$				half unit			
$\frac{1}{4}$		$\frac{1}{4}$		$\frac{1}{4}$		$\frac{1}{4}$	
$\frac{1}{8}$	$\frac{1}{8}$	$\frac{1}{8}$	$\frac{1}{8}$	$\frac{1}{8}$	$\frac{1}{8}$	$\frac{1}{8}$	$\frac{1}{8}$

Figure 4.3 Mathematical relationships between Community Playthings™ unit blocks.

Wooden unit blocks in home and group settings

Grandparents will sometimes save up to buy wooden unit blocks for their grandchildren as a major gift to last a whole childhood. Adults take great pleasure in them, too, because they are so beautiful to hold and use. A set of wooden unit blocks can lead to some marvellous family times, full of creativity on the part of both the adults and the children taking part.

Sets of wooden unit blocks can sometimes be taken on loan from toy libraries and local authorities, Early Years Partnerships, voluntary organisations and childminding networks, for accredited childminders to use in their homes.

Hollow wooden blocks

Children are often offered the large hollow blocks in the garden. This is a good way forward where space is at such a premium. It makes sense to have this provision outside, because this is the only place where there is the space to make large constructions. Some settings also use mini hollow blocks where space is an issue, but they are less stable to balance and they offer less variety of shapes.

Construction sets

It is very important to differentiate between construction kits and wooden block play:

* wooden blocks are free-standing and balancing them is an important part of their use;
* construction kits are made up of pieces that connect together in various ways, with slots, screws, nuts and bolts, and interweaving spikes.

It is best to choose only two types of construction set, one larger scale than the other. Then these can be added to, so that children have sufficient material to use. There is nothing more frustrating than not having enough blocks or pieces of the construction kit when you have an idea you want to carry out. Getting the creative idea out of your head and into the blocks or construction kit so that it becomes an act of creation depends on having enough material to do that.

Creative block play and construction play depend on:

* adults who set up the materials so that they are conducive to creative ideas and acts;
* having the materials;
* giving children freedom of choice and time to use the materials;
* giving children a broad, rich range of experiences so that they are able to develop plenty of ideas to use creatively.

Block and construction materials are expensive and will need to be carefully budgeted for. Group settings will need to include this kind of planning in their development plans. Perhaps a few blocks or construction pieces can be bought each year and so an ample set of pieces will gradually develop over the years.

There needs to be an area indoors set up for large construction experience but such that children can also take smaller construction pieces from a shelf. They may also use both types of pieces outside.

Children often prefer to construct when sitting on the floor, but it is also good to offer opportunities for working on a table.

Figures 4.4–4.6 The drummer varies the movements, creating different sounds. There are fine, gentle movements, and a flat hand makes a completely different sound. And then there is the joy of drumming and singing, both at the same time. This takes coordination. (Ockelford, 2008: Goddard-Blythe, 2004)

Non-cost materials which cultivate creativity

Sometimes situations arise spontaneously which encourage the creativity of children. During a movement session a spider let itself down on its thread and then up again. The children were fascinated and the movement session stopped in order that everyone could savour the experience.

Figure 4.7   The spider descends on its thread from the ceiling.

Figure 4.8   The spider ascends again.

Figure 4.9   The children enjoy making a shape like the legs of the spider with the practitioner. The children are not being creative here, but they are enjoying her creativity and joining in. It is important to know the difference. Children benefit from being with creative adults, but the adults need to be clear about when an idea is theirs and when it is the creation of a child.

Figure 4.10   The unexpected appearance of the spider led to a heightened interest in mini-beasts, and a display.

It is worth thinking about which materials will be costly and which won't, and planning with both in mind. Cardboard boxes, for example, cost nothing. Arranging a supply (e.g. regularly collecting boxes from a supermarket on a certain day) can bring good community links, with everyone thinking about how to help the children develop their creativity. Balancing tins and boxes of food gives a building experience for children, too. This will not harm the food, which can be put back in the cupboard later.

In both home and group care settings, with low or high budgets, we can provide opportunities for children to build and construct. However, ideally we will manage to provide some kind of wooden unit blocks and one carefully chosen construction set so that children can have deep and life-lasting experiences which will impact on their ability to be creative in this area.

Adults who become engineers, architects, theatre set designers and dramatists (creative writers in theatre) or novelists and story-writers often say how much they enjoyed playing with blocks and construction kits as children.

Famous examples would be:

* architect – Frank Lloyd Wright (whose mother was a Froebel-trained kindergarten teacher and provided him with wooden unit blocks at home);
* writer – E.E. Nesbitt, who wrote stories for children;
* writer – H.G. Wells, who wrote stories and science fiction;
* writer and poet – Robert Louis Stevenson, author of *A Child's Garden of Verses*.

The woodwork area

Woodwork, like block play and construction, is another form of material provision that offers experiences which are invaluable to children in all aspects of their development and learning, particularly their creativity.

In setting up all areas of the learning environment, whether indoors or outdoors, it is of paramount importance that children are safe. Risk assessments (Tovey, 2007) need to be made in order to make sure that children can experience full learning opportunities. Safety awareness should open up, and not close down, learning opportunities. Part of ensuring safe learning environments is for staff or those at home to think through what is necessary for this. The other part is to educate the children into thinking about their own safety and that of their friends as an important part of their learning.

The woodwork area, like every other area of provision, needs to be set up with great care. It is more important here than in other areas, however, to be able to tell at a glance which tools are not in their designated places. Children should return them here when they have finished using them.

If the area becomes very popular (there are usually some days more than others when this is so), a waiting list can be useful. Notices can be used to help children. Most of the time, when equipment is available every day, there is not much need to restrict the number of children. However, at a woodwork bench, staff clearly need to be able to work effectively with children, and children must not be crowded in case they accidentally hit a neighbour with a hammer or saw a person rather than the wood.

The woodwork area

* Everything has a place
* Little is more – which means that there are one or two hammers and saws, and one of other tools
* There is a vice to hold the wood still with safety
* The tools are easy for children to use and selected with that in mind
* Numbers are limited, with a waiting list system to ensure equality of opportunity and to make sure less assertive children have their turn
* The area is available for the whole session because it is located where an adult is always nearby
* There is a plentiful supply of easy-to-saw-and-nail wood, that is not too liable to splinter
* There are photographs on the wall of children using the area
* There is an expectation that children will use the area responsibly, and children are fully confident because they understand the clear boundaries that have been established to keep them safe
* There is discussion of safety issues as well as discussion of creative ideas coming to fruition as wooden creations between adults and children.

There are various styles of setting up woodwork areas. The important thing is that staff think carefully about how best to offer woodwork experiences to children.

Workshop area

The workshop area is usually placed near to the woodwork area. There is usually a table with basic equipment on it, such as glue, masking tape, Sellotape™, pencils for labelling or decorating, left- and right-handed scissors. There might be shelves next to the table with enticing boxes with materials that can be used for collage or model-making. Above this there needs to be a shelf to display (at child height) constructions made by the children, with labels explaining what they are about. Adults scribe what the children have told them, or children make their own marks. This gives status to the creative ideas which have become creations in the form of models.

There is less of an issue about numbers of children using the workshop area at any one time, because safety is not such a concern. Children can sit on chairs if they wish or they can stand at the table. They often choose the latter, so that they can potter about as they develop an idea. We know from research on the brain that it is difficult to think while sitting still (Goddard-Blythe, 2004). Children who are free to move are free to think fully. They may sit down if they want to be at a particular angle or in order to coordinate a movement when working to create something.

The same principles are used in every area of provision, indoors and outdoors, but every area has its particular contribution and character. Many parents and childminders now have areas that are workshops on a miniature scale. There might be a drawer in a unit at child height in the kitchen, with masking tape, pot of glue, scissors, etc. in it, and a box of straws, buttons, scraps of material, sticks, stones, etc., which the children can use while sitting at the kitchen table to create models. The workshop area also has these principles which guide its use and presentation – see box.

Workshop area

* There is a table or working surface on which children can create things
* An adult is available to support the child's creative idea and to help the child transform the idea in their head into a creation. (This is very different from the adult helping the child to make something that is an idea in the adult's head come to fruition, using the child as a vehicle for the adult's creative idea!)
* Children can see what is on offer, with clear presentation of materials
* The surfaces are easy to clean and children are not nagged about making a mess
* There is plenty of time for creative ideas to be mulled over, and no pressure to turn these into creations. The processes of creativity are valued
* When children do turn a creative idea (process) into a creation (product) and want to keep it, or take it home later, this is valued and appreciated and placed in an area with a label.

Drawing and painting

There are times when children want to paint and want to find the colours and paper available and ready to use. Their creative idea might be constrained by having to mix colours. This would slow down their flow of thoughts.

There are other times when they want to mix their own colours and to experiment. There should therefore always be the opportunity to do this. There will usually be children in a group who have an idea which they have been incubating and that is ready to come to fruition. Then they may have definite ideas about what colours they need and so will express their idea more as they want it if they can mix the colours themselves.

In the same way, when children first begin to try to set down on paper their story-writing ideas, they often need an adult to scribe for them – otherwise they get bogged down in the mechanics of writing, while the ideas that they are trying to express evaporate.

Figure 4.11   The mark-making area is next to the workshop area

Figure 4.12   This means that children can select their materials. Here the boy has chosen to draw on a strip of paper.

Figure 4.13   The strip is placed on the main drawing and other colours are used. He holds one in each hand.

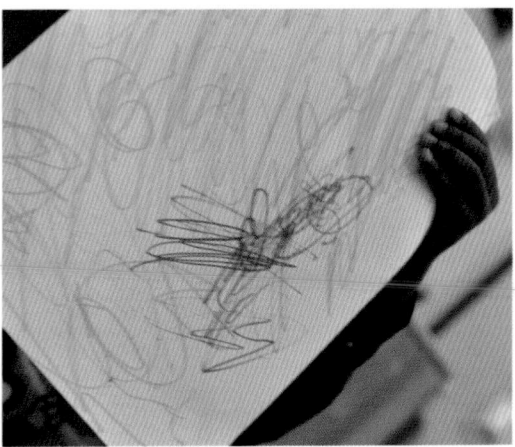

Figure 4.14   The completed drawing is shared with the adult. This is often a way for adults to tell that a child has made a finished product and that the activity was not entirely about the creative process of drawing. Often, young children are more concerned with the process than the product, but they do seem to be clear which they are involved in. He has gathered ideas at the mark-making area, simmered them, illuminated them and then hatched a creation.

Never underestimate the creativity of young children

We are inclined seriously to underestimate the creativity of children. This is probably because we seriously neglect our own creativity. Either it was never developed in us and so we don't know what it is, or we have let it go by allowing our lives to become dominated by the 'commonplace' events of life, as Isadora Duncan (1930) calls them. This is a terrible waste of brainpower.

Materials to explore

One of the things adults often recall from their childhood play is the memory of making mud pies in the garden. In most settings now there is a digging-in-the-mud patch outside, but indoors the experience is offered in a different form. Some children don't like to feel they are getting dirty and they appreciate making mixtures with 'clean' materials.

There are definite points of view about using food for play, and not all settings do so. The argument for using flour to make dough, or lentils and pasta for mixtures, is that they last a long time and only food that is beyond its sell-by date is used and so could not be used for food preparation. The argument against this is that food is precious and many people in the world are undernourished or even starving.

Puzzles and games and looking at detail

This area needs to be very clearly set out, in an attractive area. This is helpful for children who appreciate a cosy corner, where they can quietly settle at something they feel secure in doing. Games are very comforting when they are familiar and well known. This is also a good spot for an adult to sit first thing in the morning, so that children who are a bit more timid about coming to the group will feel welcomed and can find something to do that is comfortable, with an adult to support them.

Children will not become creative if they are too anxious to settle and focus and develop their own ideas. The action of threading some beads can calm children and they are then in a state to go and quietly find something that leads them into creativity. In the same way, looking at beetles and ants and spiders and stones and grass and flowers under the magnifier helps children (and adults) to concentrate and become alert to detail in ways which help creativity along.

Adults, and writers in particular, often say that if they make a cup of tea or tidy up a bit, they can feel themselves developing focus on an idea. For them, the comfortable, well-established routine seems to free the mind so that they begin to see the idea more clearly. Then they get into a state of mind where they can think more creatively.

Different personalities mean children have different styles of arriving

Some children burst through the doors when they arrive, going straight through the indoors area and out to the garden. They seem to need to move very freely before they settle into a creative focus. Other children flit from area to area, as if doing an audit of what is available. Others go straight to their favourite place, finding it to be an important start to the session. Some need their parent, carer or a member of staff (usually their key person) with them when they do this; some don't. Some look for their friend and become unsettled if he or she is absent that day.

All of these factors will influence the creativity of a child. The more we can tune into the way a child arrives in the setting, the better we can help.

Toddlers in the group setting

A two-year-old potters into the area and wants to try just about everything. He finds himself in the home area first. He finds a frying pan and a wooden spoon. When one of the older children joins him, he gives her the pan. She shows him how to pretend to fry something on the stove. He is not interested in the symbolic side of pretending to cook, and this shows in his decision to go to the next-door area and try the mixtures table.

He is a typical toddler. He sees what he wants – the seed tray full of something – and he reaches for a small strainer and puts it into the tray the older girl is using. He does what he wants because he does not understand that she regards that seed tray as hers while she is using the area! She politely restrains him and gives him a sieve, like hers, at the suggestion of a helpful adult. The adult also suggests that he might use another tray. However, he likes to be near her, so the answer is to move the tray next to the older girl. He then uses the small sieve with great concentration. He sieves into the tray, and also onto the floor.

Toddlers often come with their older brothers and sisters, and are often unwilling to leave. Many settings now take children from two to five years of age. This has huge implications for the way in which the learning environment needs to be set up. There will need to be thought given to the development of the child. The requirements of toddlers and children with special educational and complex needs are often similar. The materials offered will be similar, but need to be offered so that the children can use them without frustration for either adults or children.

If this little boy were to stay he could be directed to use the sieve outdoors in a sand tray or in the sandpit, or on a mat for the purpose on the floor. There are, in this setting, plenty of opportunities for him where he can focus and learn about the properties of materials in ways that are appropriate for him. Other children are able to use materials at their level but might need some protection or support in developing strategies to divert or re-route children like this little boy, who may unwittingly destroy their ideas and creations-in-the-making because they do not yet understand creativity in action.

Having had a positive experience with mixtures, the little boy then goes exploring to the next room. He plays the drum and the large xylophone, then plays the piano with the stick. Then he is taken home, his mother having settled his sister in.

Dressing-up clothes

Squalid dressing-up areas are unhygienic and depressing, and are badly used by the children. They should be tempting areas, which children can't wait to use. Clothes should be easy to hang up, with clear places for hats, bags, shoes and jewellery.

Clothes should be simple and have suggestion rather than rigid designation of role in the costume. Expensive dressing–up clothes from catalogues are usually too definite about the character they represent to be used for a range of stories and characters. There is nothing like simple trousers, shift tops, skirts and capes as a basic wardrobe. Children are drawn towards interesting fabrics and patterns, and appreciate some changes so that boredom does not set in.

The home corner

There should be progression in that what is suitable for a toddler needs more sophistication for children over three years of age.

Figure 4.15   The home corner in the area for children up to three years of age.

Figures 4.16–4.17 The home corner for children over three years of age.

In this chapter we have taken a preview of how the learning environment indoors is set up before the arrival of the children and their families. We have also noted that there will be different ways of coming into the setting, reflecting the personality of each child. We have looked at some but not all areas of provision, but the principles and practical strategies outlined are part of a holistic approach and so apply to all areas indoors and in the garden.

Reflective questions

Audit the material provision indoors and outdoors. Are you offering children **narrow activities, or open-ended experiences**? How much choice do they have in the way they use materials? Can they choose what they do and can they select which areas they want to be in?

It is important to offer children open-ended experiences so that play, creativity and imagination are cultivated. Choose an area (such as wooden block play or paint) and organise using this chapter to do so.

Observe children in the area.

Useful texts

Core Experiences for the Early Years Foundation Stage 2009,
    Kate Greenaway Nursery School and Children's Centre, available from
    www.early-education.org.uk
A Place to Learn: Developing a Stimulating Learning Environment (2003)
    Lewisham Early Years Advice and Resource Network (LEARN)

5 Creating an environment – into the garden

Just outside the door

We saw in the last chapter that children vary in the way in which they make the daily transition from home and journey into the group setting. Some seem to come through the door and positively burst into action, often heading straight for the garden, the adult standing by supportively, without constraining their freedom of movement. Other children meander about when they arrive, as if they are waiting to see what's on offer. This, we have seen, is particularly typical of younger children and toddlers. After all, they have not yet built up enough life experience to know what, out of all the rich choices, they find most interesting and satisfying. They need to go exploring and to 'find something of interest' (Carr, 1999).

There are children who like to be with an adult and don't settle easily unless they can read a book or do something quiet and focused together with their parent, carer or one of the staff. They often stay indoors for a bit. Others just appreciate having an adult nearby; the mere presence of an adult gives them sufficient security. There are children who like to stay indoors at first, and there are children who like to be outdoors at first.

In a well-prepared learning environment, in either home care or a group setting, children are able to choose what is best for them as they settle in their own individual way into a day of developing, learning and hopefully being creative. In the home and group settings in this book, children's creativity is being cultivated to the full. We saw in an earlier chapter that in order to be creative, children need both to feel part of things and to feel that they are a separate person with their own ideas.

It is important to set up both the indoor and outdoor areas with these different personalities in mind, so that every child will feel comfortable about using both rooms and the outside area. Children need to feel a sense of belonging and that they are themselves, in order that their creativity can develop.

Figure 5.1 The adult and child are engaged in a game with the ball. The bowling is overarm.

In one of the settings, the first areas of provision that children will see as they go outside are:

* an area set up as an office;
* a table with a small construction kit;
* a cosy place to look at books under a tree, with bushes and cushions;
* a self-service drinks table;
* Wellington boots and a waterproof clothing trolley.

It is important that all areas of provision are offered in ways that the children can readily access. Children appreciating adult company or feeling a need for the security of sitting and doing something familiar will be likely to use the office and construction kit. Children needing larger-scale physical action might note the waterproof wear on the trolley and surge on outwards to run about before deciding what to do. This is not unusual for children who have been constrained in the freedom of their movement in a small home with no garden or after travelling in a car. Most of the children attending the settings in this book are very local, living in flats.

Figure 5.2 Freedom of movement is good for brain development. Children, once they are experienced, think up many creative ways to hang from, move across and climb on climbing frames.

Children may also be noting for later use the wooden guttering and poles from which they can make waterfalls and gushing, spurting and moving water. These are all signals to the children that they can get messy and wet.

Further into the garden

As they venture further into the garden, they find a challenging climbing frame and plenty of space to run about unconstrained and also places which challenge the direction in which they run (straight or circular running) and which require more coordination.

Figures 5.3–5.5 The boys chase each other around the bamboo and then hold it, watching it swing back as they release hold. They change direction and begin to coordinate their movements, meeting at the place where they always swing the bamboo sticks.

Figure 5.6   The play scenario attracts other children, who join in the chasing but not the swinging of the bamboo.

Figure 5.7   The swinging becomes rather rougher and the adult, who has been observing nearby, joins the play and gently encourages their interest in playing together with the wheeled vehicles rather than swinging the bamboo. It is important that practitioners observe children at play, so that they can help them. The important thing here was the children's enjoyment of coordinating their movements. They were easily redirected to do this on wheels rather than damaging the bamboo with too much pulling.

As children move further into the garden, with their friends, with or without an adult, they encounter another table with books, a sandpit shaded from too much sun, wind or rain, and quiet places to sit, where stories are told and dances and songs take place whenever the weather permits in group times at the end of the session.

There are pictures and labels of the typical wildlife found in the well-placed bushes in the middle and at the bottom of the garden. Children are often found pausing between play episodes, when they are in transition to their next focus, looking with quiet interest at these.

Figure 5.8   The girl is looking at the picture of the bird with her key person and they have a conversation about birds they see and what birds do.

Children who are well established in the setting know that once the to and fro of the start of the day is over, staff will help them to take out the wheeled vehicles and the large hollow blocks. Doing this together saves the staff some physical energy, because the children help. It also encourages the children to think about how they might use the different vehicles, and in developing their ideas they move into a creative mode.

Books, books everywhere

Wherever the children go indoors and outdoors they need to find books. Books are relevant to the area of material provision they support and also pick up on current interests of clusters of children or individual children. For example, there are books about art in the painting area.

Each room also has a story area with books in it. This can be used for wooden unit block play in one room and for stories with props.

Seeing other people's ideas for stories, songs and poems (fiction) and factual books (non-fiction) helps children to see new and creative possibilities. They use what they find, rearrange, alter, adapt ideas that other people have, for their own stories, models, constructions, dances, music, paintings and drawings and scientific theorising.

In later chapters we shall find that, time and again, books are very important in cultivating creativity. They help us to explore with the children:

* how to do things;
* how to use techniques;
* how to find information: for example, about dinosaurs.

What have we found out about cultivating creativity so far?

Creativity is not a gift that we are born with. Creativity is part of everyone's development and learning. Unless it is helped along and supported, actively encouraged and cultivated, the possibilities for it to develop can be extinguished or constrained.

We have found three kinds of creativity:

1. everyday creativity;
2. specialist creativity;
3. world-shattering creativity.

Most creativity is of the first kind, so that is the main focus of this book. Very little is of the last kind. Specialists, however, are very influential in the impact they have on our daily lives through their creativity. We sometimes know their names, but often we don't.

Some people are very good at interpreting other people's creative ideas. Good performers do this. Other people are better at both creating ideas and taking them to fruition, turning them into creations. Creative people use their own ideas when they do this. Of course, there are often overlaps: for example, when the creator and performer are one and the same person.

Creative people do not have to be difficult and temperamental – this is not a necessary condition in order for someone to be creative. Most creative people are well balanced, which is why they are able to develop their ideas and thoughts sufficiently to carry them through to fruition, with a creation as the result. Jung, the famous psychologist, thought that being neurotic was 'the most formidable obstacle to creation' (in Howkins, 2001: 5).

We find creativity of different kinds. Sometimes it is entirely in the way we use our senses and movements. At other times, it is in the way we develop and use symbols of all kinds. Symbols stand for something else. Those who, for one reason or another, cannot develop symbolic creativity can still be creative in ways which use the senses and movements. Creativity develops in layers.

Creative people have new ideas, but this doesn't make them revolutionaries. It means they are using their adaptive human intelligence. Seeing new ways of doing things is part of intelligent behaviour. It is central to creativity. Creativity is a high-level aspect of thinking because it shows depth of:

* process (developing the idea inside your mind); and
* product (outward creation emerging from the idea).

What has setting up the environment got to do with cultivating creativity?

Creativity doesn't just happen. Just as babies do not learn to speak or sign unless they are spoken to, in the same way babies, toddlers and young children do not develop creativity without help. It might be argued that it is more important to learn to speak or sign than it is to be a creative person. In some ways this is true. People who cannot communicate with others are in great difficulty. Neither is thinking at a sophisticated level possible without language. However, creativity takes the commonplace out of life and makes life satisfying and fulfilling. It develops the ability for thinking, because it is about developing ideas and hatching them into creations. To do this, thinking has to be flexible, has to adapt, must be able to rearrange ideas and to follow ideas through without losing them on the way. Creativity is hard work.

Figure 5.9   The girls play together in the sand, creating different ways of adding to their sandcastles, knocking them down and rearranging them. Making new connections and rearranging things are at the heart of creativity.

People who carry creative experiences inside them live more fully. They have more control over what happens to them because they have dispositions towards life which make them full of adventure, and they both solve and generate problems in order to find better ways of doing things. They are less likely to be passive people who depend on others to do their thinking for them, waiting for instructions and anxious about whether they are pleasing their instructors or angry at their lack of personal power.

We can see that when the children enter the learning environments in this book, whether in home care or group settings, those environments have been set up to cultivate their creativity.

In this chapter, we have seen that, in order to be creative, children need to:

* choose and make decisions
* find a wide range of experiences
* be challenged with problems to solve
* take risks and have adventures in learning
* find a predictable, safe environment where there are clear boundaries
* be supported by informed, highly trained staff (who should be led by graduate-trained teachers)
* learn how to use the materials at the level appropriate for them
* be listened to
* be encouraged to share their emerging thoughts
* find their creations valued and discussed with them
* be respected when they are concentrating on an idea
* find that adults protect their personal space when they need to focus
* find that adults are good companions when they are finding a focus
* be given help when they ask for it
* be given help when they are struggling, so that they don't give up
* be allowed to develop their own ideas, and adults don't take them over
* be with adults who support their creative ideas
* see that their parents are partners with the staff.

Reflective questions

How do you organise the ways in which children use the garden in your setting? Can they go immediately into the garden when they arrive? Can they go out in all weathers? Can they make dens? How much is the garden part of the learning environment, and do you pay as much attention to it as to the indoor environment?

Useful texts

Milchen, K. (2010) The Urban Forest School: Reconnecting with nature through Froebelian pedagogy, early childhood practice. *The Journal for Multi-Professional Partnerships*, Vol. 11, Nos. 1 and 2, pp. 106–117.

Tovey, H. (2007) *Playing Outdoors: Spaces and Places, Risk and Challenge*. Open University Press: Maidenhead.

6 Including everyone – the beginnings of creativity

Emergent creativity

There is often a view that children can be creative only after they have acquired certain techniques that enable them to make creations. For this reason, babies are often not thought of as capable of being creative. There are several problems with this point of view.

First, educators who say this do not distinguish between:

* knowing about the beginnings and early emergent signs of creativity in babies or those who for one reason or another (early traumatic experiences, ill health, special educational needs, disabilities or complex needs) are later in developing their creativity;
* being creative;
* making a creation.

Their view focuses only on children's ability to make a creation that complies with conventional criteria of the culture. This ignores the processes of creativity which lead to creation.

Second, when this view is taken, creativity is really seen as the way in which the child learns a craft or skills, with the techniques needed being directly taught. The adult gives the child the skills and technical know-how and then the child is free to be creative. This is a linear view of creativity and suggests that a child can be creative only if they are skilled enough to make creations. It does not value the individual creativity of the child, which involves the creative thinking that goes on in the child's mind.

Third, it sees creativity as a skilled craft (usually emphasising the arts and not the humanities or sciences), as an ability to create things according to the conventions of cultural expectations and requirements.

Being creative is an attitude of mind, which if developed early supports us through our lives

In this book we take a different view. Creativity is thought of as an umbrella word, with three things under it, each of equal importance:

1. emergent beginnings of creativity;
2. being a creative learner (a process);
3. making creations (products).

These do not develop in a linear way, although the emergent beginnings inevitably come first. Being a creative learner is a state of mind throughout life if the beginnings are established. Some of us are more inclined to make products (creations) than others. Some of us make creative products that change the world. Some of us make creative products that show great expertise, and help knowledge and understanding to develop in important but often small ways. Some of us make everyday creative products that increase the satisfaction and fulfilment of our lives in personal and individual ways.

Creativity in babies begins through relationships with particular people and through non-verbal communication. It also begins with learning through the senses and the sixth sense of movement feedback (embodiment, which brings a sense of self and connectedness with others). Flo Longhorn (1988), in her pioneering work with children with complex needs, points out that a diverse range of people need a particular emphasis on multi-sensory learning at various points in their lives. These include:

* babies;
* premature babies;
* under-stimulated children (physical, emotional and intellectual neglect);
* people with failing senses (going deaf or blind);
* someone who has been in a coma;
* older people;
* people in hospital settings;
* those rejoining a community after leaving a hospital setting;
* children with specific learning difficulties;
* people undergoing therapeutic difficulties. (Longhorn, 1988: 18–19)

Through multi-sensory experiences in companionship and interactions with people they love, children develop a sense of embodiment which gives them a sense of self. The beginnings of creativity emerge in the way that very young babies see themselves as the cause of making things happen and making people behave in certain ways. Autonomy and a sense of our own agency are crucial to multi-sensory experience. Predicting and anticipating are a part of this.

We can encourage these glimmerings of the creative self in babies, right from the start, by helping them to see the impact of what they do. A classic example is Magda, who is sitting in her high chair. She is given a rusk to keep her busy while her mother prepares the meal by heating it. Magda bangs the rusk on the tray and pauses to listen to the different sounds – on the edge, on top, on the top of her head.

Here we see **variation** on the same action – banging.

Then she picks at the rusk and notices how it crumbles a bit. She likes the crumbs and drops them onto the tray. She stirs them about in a circular movement and looks at her mother for her reaction. Her mother says, 'You're a mucky thing, aren't you? Stirring your rusk round and round', making the action with her arm. 'Yes! You're a messy girl, you are!' This is said in a jovial tone. Magda returns to her stirring gleefully.

Her mother has responded in an important way. She has called attention to the pattern Magda has made. She has shown Magda what she has done. Magda looks at the round pattern and does it again. This encourages her to predict and anticipate the fact that a particular action leads to a particular pattern with the crumbs. Having a sense of intention, as these cause-and-effect relationships develop, will in the future help Magda to develop creative ideas which she will have some control over and at times will manage to turn into creations.

Let's look at the beginnings of becoming a creative learner in more detail.

Lynne Murray and Liz Andrews show us how, in the second and third months of life, babies enjoy face-to-face play:

> Face-to-face play with babies in the second and third months can seem like a musical duet, and distinct phrases when the baby's initiative is taken up by the parent who, quite unconsciously, mirrors, builds on and develops the baby's original communication. Play is intimate, and concerns nothing but the feelings and expressions of the two partners. The parents' mirroring is a very immediate way of conveying their acceptance of the baby, and it can both affirm and enrich the baby's experience.
>
> (Murray and Andrews, 2000: 52)

Time and again in this book we return to the importance of adults tuning into the child's spontaneous initiatives, efforts to communicate and intentions (Bruce and Spratt, 2011). Joey looks at his mother and moves as his face changes expression. When we see a baby move in a very lively way while looking intently at us, and perhaps cooing at us, too, we need to tune in at once. We can make a 'musical duet' together. Trevarthen (1998) talks about these early two-way conversations without words as 'proto-conversations'.

As these become well established, Murray and Andrews show how the baby uses the known and familiar, predictable structure to anticipate and feel a sense of agency and control over events:

> Common examples are body games, such as 'round and round the garden' or even the very simple routines, like the looming in of the partner's face to touch the baby's tummy. These may start gently, the baby quite seriously watching the partner's face; then the partner gradually helps to build up the sense of anticipation, holding the baby's gaze and monitoring her readiness throughout, using voice, facial expression and widening of the eyes to mark the imminent arrival of the final climax, when the high point of emotion is shared together. In this way, the face-to-face conversations develop from simply focusing on what the baby may be feeling or thinking, to having a definite structure and topic.
>
> (Murray and Andrews, 2000: 63)

Topics are often 'coo and boo' games and gradually, from three months typically, involve the wider world of objects, such as dummies and rattles.

Babies are born with the possibility to be both problem solvers and problem generators (Karmiloff-Smith, 1992). Both require creative learning, although generating problems emphasises this more. As we have noted in other parts of the book, learning through a multi-sensory world and from their own movements is crucial to babies. Alison Gopnik, Andrew Meltzoff and Patricia Kuhl (1999) describe this sense of embodiment in the developing sense of self (me, myself and I) and suggest that:

> There is nothing more personal, more part of you, than this internal sense you have of your own body, your expressions and movements, your aches and tickles. And yet from the time we are born, we seem to link this deeply personal self to the bodily movements of other people, movements we can only see and not feel. Nature ingeniously gives us a jump start on the Other Minds problem. We know, quite directly, that we are like other people and they are like us.
>
> (Gopnik *et al.*, 1999: 30)

Babies' sense of embodiment connects with the sense that other people are like them. They have a sense of connection with other people, which bypasses spoken or signed language and opens up the beginnings of creative learning.

Predicting, anticipating and controlling – the beginnings of creativity

One of the ways in which we know that babies have made an important start in realising they are creative learners is observing their joy, typically after the first two months of their lives, in being able to predict, anticipate and control. They revel in their sense of agency, through which they realise there is a connection between what they do and how people react. They widen this exciting realisation and begin to apply it to objects, too. They become fascinated by novelty. It is as if they are asking themselves the question, 'Do people and things always react in the same way when I do this or that?'

There are many psychological tests with babies which are based on the look of surprise when a baby's prediction does not turn out as expected (Goswami, 1998). If things do turn out as expected time and time again, then the baby becomes bored and moves to something else.

Novelty, making new connections and variations on a theme – emergent creativity

Novelty and variations on a theme are at the heart of the baby becoming a creative learner, but it is the baby who needs to control this, because only the baby has a sense of what will happen. The adult does not know what the baby's predictions are. The adult can help by being a tuned-in partner in the play. Offering to play and being sensitive to the baby's mood is important at times. Responding to the baby's spontaneous requests to play is important at other times.

Throughout our lives we make connections with our previous experiences. We make links between things that were not previously linked.

The beginnings of creative learning emerge out of the ideas babies have from birth. Gopnik *et al.* (1999) suggest that they use these to learn more, elaborating what they know in the light of their experiences with people and the physical world they are introduced to by people.

We can see how our knowledge emerges from the ideas we start out with, our ability to learn and our interactions with other people (Gopnik *et al.*, 1999: 206). They point out that in evolutionary terms, the dangers linked with babies, toddlers and young children being explorers are offset by the benefits of the beginnings of a life-long possibility for creative, thinking, autonomous learning. As they develop their sense of embodied self and being an active agent in producing causes for things to happen, and observing the effects of their actions on people and objects, they learn about the way things disappear, and how to classify and organise what they know into concepts that help them to think more deeply.

Figure 6.1   The baby is playing with a Treasure Basket (developed by Elinor Goldschmied, a Froebelian pioneer of the education of babies and toddlers). The baby is exploring the objects in a very systematic way.

By the time they can sit, babies:

> will systematically examine a new object with every sense they have at their command (including taste, of course).

(Gopnik et al., 1999: 88)

By the end of their first year they typically vary what they do with an object, perhaps tapping gently, then banging fiercely. As toddlers, they look for the unexpected in an object, as if fascinated, and sort things into piles which have, amazingly, to the tuned-in observer, some consistent logic in them (Gopnik *et al.*, 1999). This kind of creative thinking is significant for human learning. Other animals cannot manage creative thinking of this depth.

Cultural variations

Of course, as we would expect, there are cultural variations and great diversities in the kinds of creative learning that develop in babies, toddlers and young children, because people in different cultures and contexts cultivate creativity (or don't cultivate creativity) in very different ways.

For example, Korean parents talking with their babies emphasise problem solving, such as how to get an out-of-reach toy, whereas English-speaking parents talk about the categories of objects more, such as, 'Here's your cup.' But by the age of two years, Korean children understand all about the categories of objects and English-speaking toddlers understand the actions of people and objects.

Babies seem to learn about the external world in much the way they learn about other minds. They start out with some crucial assumptions, assumptions that seem to be built in. But, just as important, they are endowed with powerful abilities to learn and even more powerful motivations (Gopnik *et al.*, 1999: 91).

Movement patterns and creative beginnings

John Matthews (2003) mentions the repertoire of movement patterns (schemas) available to babies, which become elaborated as the baby begins to experiment and receive feedback from people and objects.

> Joel, at just over six months, is lying on his stomach on a purple carpet. He regurgitates some milk onto the carpet in front of him, presenting a contrasting white, circular patch before his eyes. He reaches his fingers into this irresistible visual target and makes a scratching movement. He hears his fingers scratching into the carpet and seems to be interested in the changes he is causing to take place.

(Matthews, 2003: 52)

Gradually, babies begin to realise that they can make marks with paint, crayons, milk on their food tray. Earlier in the chapter, we saw how Magda made a trajectory pathway through the pile of crumbs on her high-chair tray.

We find the beginnings of creativity in the way babies explore:

* a sense of embodiment – movement feedback;
* seeing others move and realising they are people who move like me;
* face-to-face interactions between baby and a loved person;
* predictable forms of play – tickle games or coo-and-boo responses;
* cause and effect – I did that;
* does that happen every time I do that? Predicting and anticipating;
* I can make things happen and people do things, too – sense of agency; variations and novelty.

Special educational needs, disabilities and complex needs – looking for signs of emergent creativity

Throughout this book there are examples of children engaged in creative thinking and acts of creation. Among these are children with special educational needs and disabilities. They are not easy to spot, because when children feel included they do not stand out. They belong and are part of their community.

The submarine and the Viking ship

When he was about seven years of age, Chris made a Viking boat out of coloured pipe cleaners. It happened quite quickly. He had been learning about Vikings at school, but this happened during the holidays. He was given the packet of pipe cleaners as a gift and he picked his way through them, then began twisting them with intense concentration. The next thing anyone knew, he had made a Viking ship.

Children are sometimes a little taken aback by their creations. It is as if they can hardly believe what they have created. Chris sat looking at it. The adult did not say, 'What is it?' This might have been rather deflating for him. Instead she said, 'That's an intricate construction. I'd love to know more about it.' He told her it was a Viking ship. She could see this at once and she admired the different features. She put it in her glass-fronted bookcase in front of some books. It stayed there for years. It is still there now! It is valued, appreciated and treasured.

David watched this scene with interest. He is younger than his brother. Four years later, when he was nine years old, he arrived at the house with a huge construction made of wood. It was painted grey. His father had helped him to make it – holding the wood still and making sure the nails were well placed to bang them in with the hammer without bending. He announced, 'I made you a submarine.' He moved swiftly to the glass-fronted bookcase, clearly expecting a place to be found for it. A shelf was quickly cleared of books and the submarine just fitted onto it. David looked at it with pride and muttered, with deep satisfaction, 'Boat, like my brother.'

For four years, he had been incubating the idea. He needed time for the idea to take root, to gather his thoughts, to find a form for them and then to take them into a tangible shape as a submarine. It took four years to:

* prepare;
* incubate;
* illuminate;
* hatch.

Figure 6.2 The boy is dancing without music, using his own rhythms, in tune with his body.

Figures 6.3–6.4 He is enjoying interacting with the practitioner (a conversation in movement rather than in words). Other children take pleasure in this 'movement conversation', too.

It is easy to underestimate the time it takes for children to develop a creative idea, especially those children with disabilities. At a dance lesson at RNIB Redhill College, attended by further education students with complex needs, of which visual disability was dominant, it was evident that the need to take the time to cultivate creativity was built into the way the timetable had been developed. The dance ideas were developed with staff tuning into the individual dance ideas of each student. One student loved to put her arms out, as in second-position ballet, and really used the music to give expression to her movement. Staff had helped her to decide where she should place herself, when she should use her dance motif, and when she should walk across the dance floor. Another student twirled across the room, rotating with his arm out.

Including everyone in creativity

Stuart Jackson was a student of the RNIB College, attending the life skills programme in literacy, numeracy, mobility, Braille and self-help skills. He joined the S.T.E.P. (Saburo Teshigawara Education Project) and toured with the dance company in Helsinki and other countries, finishing with a performance at the Sadler's Wells Theatre in London. This example highlights the point made in the first chapter, that anyone can be creative. The kind of dance improvisations Stuart had been encouraged to develop at the RNIB College were seen by the director of the dance company, who had invited him to join the company.

It is important to recognise that creativity is possible in every human being. Music, dance and the visual arts are areas where this often emerges, because these do not depend on verbal or signed languages. This does not mean that these forms of the arts are easier than the humanities or sciences. But they are different. They do not need words. They open up important areas of ourselves which help us to live very fully.

Children with special educational needs, disabilities and complex needs have the same requirements as other children in relation to how adults can help them to cultivate their creativity. They need:

* people who believe they can be creative;
* a supportive setting and learning environment;
* to be encouraged to develop their play;
* a consistent environment with a rich range of materials;
* experiences offered which are interesting to them;
* to be encouraged to make decisions and choices;
* to be given personal space to develop their ideas;
* to be offered music, dance, artistic experiences in particular because these do not depend on verbal or signed languages;
* to be offered song, poetry, story and real first-hand experiences of food preparation, shopping, etc.;
* to be talked with (not at) such that the adult shows genuine interest in what the child communicates.

One area that tends to be challenging for some (but not by any means all) children with disabilities is imagination. For example, children with autism see the world literally. Peter McKellar (1957) sees the imagination as the way that we rearrange our experiences and knowledge in new and often rather fascinating ways. In order to do this, we form an image in our minds – a mental image. This can be:

* auditory – sound;
* visual – sight;
* tactile – touch;
* olfactory – smell;
* taste;
* kinaesthetic – movement feedback.

Some children with disabilities may have difficulty with some of these senses because of a sensory impairment such as hearing or visual impairment. Robert Orr (2003) suggests that the sense of smell is very important for children with complex needs.

Becoming imaginative – it's all in the head

Mental images are an important part of developing the ability to be a symbol user. When children represent things, they use their experiences and externalise them, instead of keeping them inside as private images. Matthew (three years) loved to watch diggers at work. It was no surprise that he chose to draw one. Kit (four years) was fascinated by Tudor ships and he decided to draw the *Mary Rose*.

We do not always find out the mental imagery of children, precisely because it is inside their head! But this doesn't mean that it isn't there.

Another important aspect of becoming a symbol user is imitation. This is another way of rearranging our experiences. Imitation is not copying. When we copy we do exactly the same as the person or thing we copy. When we imitate, we take an idea and incorporate it into our own ideas, using it as a resource.

Again, children with special educational needs, disabilities and complex needs are often able to imitate, taking other people's ideas and making them their own.

Pretending is more difficult, but often role-play is helpful here. Anne, parent of Megan, a ten-year-old with learning difficulties, found that her daughter kept having temper tantrums when she arrived home, tired, at the end of a day spent in her early years setting. She suggested that she and her daughter act a story called 'Coming home'. She offered to be the 'little girl' and invited Megan to be the 'mother'. Megan agreed, with enthusiasm. They had an enjoyable time deciding on their costumes and dressed up as their characters. The 'mother' talked, imitating Anne's way of talking, and the 'child' had a full-scale temper tantrum.

Megan looked aghast. She was shocked. It helped her to see how her mother felt. She began to look at what was happening from her mother's viewpoint. Megan began to develop the play, making further events in the story, such as being bad-tempered at meal times, or going to bed, or wanting sweets when out shopping. She couldn't manage to play such scenarios with dolls or small-world play – she could manage it only if she had her mother playing with her in partnership and could direct Anne in the play.

Anne did not try to force her into small-world play or doll play because she could see that the play would deepen into free-flow play if she allowed herself to become Megan's play prop and carry out her own creative 'script'.

We often find that children with learning difficulties and disabilities develop pretend play much later, sometimes, as we see with Megan, many years later than most children. It is important therefore to continue to give them the kind of learning environment which encourages its development.

Piaget (1952) thought that in order for symbol use to develop, children need to:

* ✳ make images in their minds;
* ✳ imitate (rather than copy);
* ✳ pretend in their play.

In this book we keep emphasising the way that free-flowing play (Bruce, 1991), with its flexible, mobile, adaptive features, contributes to creative ideas developing. As images become increasingly mobile and connected, deeper layers of creative thinking become possible. When creative thinking is well under way, then creations may begin to form. The encouraging thing from the point of view of children with complex needs is that the ability to pretend is not essential to creative thinking. Symbolic creativity is one kind of creativity, but not the only one. Children can be original in other ways, too.

Having an intention

We have seen in the earlier part of the book that the glimmerings of having an intention are part of the journey into creativity. It is therefore useful to observe babies to see how they are developing the early processes that emerge before symbol use is present. In the strict and pure sense, the creator has to intend to create something, but it seems to be the case that, in its beginnings, the move into being creative may simply mean having an awareness that something is happening which they want to happen; they can't express it in words or signs.

Abraham Maslow (1973: 59) writes about having what he calls 'peak experiences'. These are times when things are experienced very intensely and such that the child or adult experiencing them is aware that something special is happening to them, in deep and satisfying ways. Maslow thought that these moments brought together creativeness and a sense of self.

In this chapter we have seen that being a creative learner is preceded by signs of the emergent beginnings of creativity. It is a long process. Babies are at the beginning of it, and so are some of the children we work or live with who have special educational needs, disabilities and complex needs, or who are recovering from illnesses or traumatic experiences.

Reflective questions

Babies love action songs, such as 'Round and round the garden like a teddy bear'. Select some songs and sing them with a baby. How does the baby respond? How important is your relationship with the baby in bringing enjoyment together? Does the baby watch carefully, respond by anticipating, giggling? Evaluate what you observe in this 'conversation' and play.

Useful texts

Bruce, T. (2011) *Learning Through Play: Babies, Toddlers and the Foundation Years, 2nd Edition*. Hodder Education: London.

Bruce, T. And Spratt, J. (2011) *Essentials of Communication, Language and Literacy, 2nd Edition*. Sage: London (see the chapters on babies and early songs and finger rhymes and actions).

Forbes, R. (2004) *Beginning to Play from Birth to Three*. Open University Press: Maidenhead.

Ockelford, A. (1996) All Join In: A Framework for making music with children and young people who are visually impaired and have learning difficulties. RNIB: Peterborough (This is also invaluable for use with any babies, toddlers and young children).

Cultivating creativity in toddlers

7

We have seen in earlier chapters that creativity is about both being a separate individual and feeling connected to others, with a sense of belonging to a group and culture. Children who are helped to develop their unique and personal creations will also be participating in the cultural context in which they grow up. In this way they will come to know themselves as creative people and also be competent in interpreting and using the creations which become the conventions of the culture.

Toddlers are at an exciting point in their lives, because they are beginning to realise that they are separate and different from other people, although their need to belong is strong. Like teenagers, they are fiercely independent, but they also need support and guidance.

Figures 7.1–7.2   The toddler wants to jump in the puddle, but he does not yet have the coordination to do this. He enjoys watching children who can make patterns and splash in the water by jumping. Young children learn a huge amount from being in the company of older children when the atmosphere created by adults is supportive, and the community is one in which everyone helps others to be of their best. In a later chapter, there is a photograph of an older child jumping in this puddle with great style, skill and creativity. The toddler seen here watches the older boy with admiration (see page 86 to see how the older boy splashes in a puddle).

They are also beginning to become symbol users. This means that they are beginning to realise that they can make one thing stand for another, whether or not it is present.

The play of toddlers is very literal, and not far removed from the real situation. For example, much of the play throughout the world is about food preparation and the sharing of meals. In recent years, mobile phone play has become a typical subject in toddler play scenarios. Toddlers are just beginning, as they walk and talk, to develop pretend play. This means they are beginning to move away from the here and now, but they use their real experiences to do this. The richer the experiences, the more they have that can be used as a resource in their play, pretend and imagination.

Figure 7.3 Chatting to the cook about how he helped her to prepare the meal (which is a daily event in this nursery school), he is reminded of the procedures and sequences and this is likely to be used in his pretend-play scenarios.

Figure 7.4   The girls are eating broccoli. Learning about different vegetables and how they are cooked is something which will show up in their play scenarios. Children use their first-hand experiences in their play.

Figure 7.5   The practitioner and child are engaged in a conversation about the meal. Walking, talking and pretending develop at the same time. The conversations that children have with adults and other children support the images which are then used in pretend play.

Personal symbols and creativity

Throughout their lives, creative people develop their own personal symbols. They never lose the ability to do this. People who are not creative either never develop this aspect of living to any great extent or lose the ability as early childhood fades. This leads to the living of commonplace lives, as Isadora Duncan describes. This means that their lives are not deeply satisfying in the way that they could be.

When toddlers are helped to develop their personal symbols, they find this very exciting. For example, in a group setting a bunch of two- and three-year-olds had visited the local shops and one of the children had fallen in love with the adult's rucksack into which the shopping had been put. The staff decided to set up a supermarket in the room. They had a bag area, where children could choose what to carry their shopping in. They put out tins and wooden beads, and scrunched up newspaper for the children to buy pretend vegetables and fruit.

One of the children had been fascinated with the credit card and the way it was swiped at the computer at the pay desk. The adult made some cards which were the same size as the credit cards and asked the children to sign them, showing them her credit card. This really took off, with all the children wanting credit cards to 'sign' with scribble. This then led to children needing wallets and purses in which to put their credit cards. One child wanted some money. A box of counters was found in the cupboard and children could use these as pretend money.

Within minutes the room and outdoor area were swarming with children with bags containing purses, money and credit cards. There was a great deal of opening and shutting of bags, and walking about. The most popular bags were the rucksacks.

The pay desk was hectic with activity. Toddlers love queues. They also enjoyed taking the supermarket baskets and filling them with 'shopping' and then unloading them at the pay desk. There was a collection of paper bags into which children could put their pretend fruit and vegetables. The adult, Judy, based herself at the pay desk in order to support the 'shopkeeper' in putting the goods into plastic carrier bags and swiping the credit cards with gusto. The cash register was a plastic replica bought from a toy catalogue and kept for situations such as this.

Observing the way in which children developed their personal symbols during this free-flow play scenario was illuminating. One child chose to wear a hat. Another selected the pink rucksack and walked around the garden with it on her back, pushing her 'baby' in the pram. When she came inside she was allowed to bring the pushchair and delighted in putting her purchases on the rack under the chair.

Toddlers need adult support in developing their creativity

As always, the adult support was of central importance in cultivating the creative ideas of these children. If the little girl had not been allowed to bring the pushchair inside, although there is a rule that vehicles may not be brought indoors, her play and the creative ideas that were part of it would have faded and vanished.

If adults had moved in on the children's play too much, they would have turned it into their story with the children as actors in it. Instead they cultivated the children's creative ideas by giving them open-ended props as suggestions, such as the cards for credit cards, newspaper balls as fruit and vegetables, bags and a commercial toy computer cash register.

When children are just beginning to develop symbolic creative ideas, they need props to help them sustain their ideas. Toddlers are often not too fussy about how realistic these look, as we saw with the credit cards and newspaper food. However, they do like to use real things as well, such as the rucksacks. These seem to serve as realistic anchors to their creative ideas as they free-flow play. This might be why they are such fierce possessors of some objects.

For toddlers, losing a play prop means losing the creative moment in the free-flow play. Certainly fierce fights developed over the supermarket baskets, until more arrived from other rooms in the setting. The creative ideas in the play of toddlers can be quickly destroyed when disputes over property break out. Sharing and taking turns are unreasonable requests on the part of adults in such situations. With teamwork, more props can usually be provided.

There are recurring themes in children's play. Food preparation and related subjects are by far the most popular play scenarios among toddlers around the world. If adults plan resources with this in mind, potential fights can be kept to a minimum. Bags, hats, props to symbolise money, paper bags, prams and a cash register are likely to be needed very regularly in a group of toddlers.

Lauren (eighteen months) enjoys playing shops at home with her three-year-old sister, Kim-Anh. Her sister initiates the play and she willingly follows. Kim-Anh decides that Lauren needs a shopping basket, so she takes her by the hand to find one. Lauren, who probably doesn't realise that she is 'playing shops', takes the basket, with the objects Kim-Anh puts into it, into the other room as directed by her sister. She looks pleased to hold the basket. Kim-Anh sits her down next to the cash desk and encourages her to check out her shopping. She swipes each item that she takes from Lauren.

Older children are often the ones who introduce toddlers to dramatic play that contains the beginnings of creative thinking in relation to literature and stories. Lauren is happy to take part in the shop play, and once she is at the checkout counter is a willing participant. She knows that you have to give objects to the person sitting at the desk and that you get them back to put in your basket.

However, it is evident from her body movement and involvement in what she is doing (Laevers, 1994) that she enjoys the food-preparation play more. This is often the first kind of role-play that toddlers actively take part in.

A recent arrival, fast taking over from the traditional telephone play of toddlers, is mobile phone play (Christiansen, 2002). Lauren needs a realistic prop and shows that she knows you have to press buttons and then listen. Phones are cultural artefacts of great importance for modern toddlers growing up in the UK.

Lauren also plays with dolls and shows her doll to her mother and then her father. Toddlers delight in giving and then taking back objects. Interestingly, she seems to understand that in order to play with the doll's house she needs a doll small enough to fit into its rooms, so she rejects the larger doll and finds a smaller one. She is more interested in putting the doll in and out than anything else. She is not yet ready to make her own story about the doll who lives in the house.

Nevertheless, it is remarkable to think that she has only recently started to walk, talk and pretend, and yet she is already showing a range of creative thinking in early form.

* She is beginning to learn about playing shops with her sister.
* She is confident about pretending to prepare food.
* She is confident about pretending to use a mobile phone.
* She knows some dolls fit in doll's houses.

Her parents, without consciously realising it, are putting into action the strategies in the box below, and showing her the sensitivity that is crucial to her creative development. Her father realises she is tiring after her burst of food-preparation play, shop play and doll's house play, and encourages her to have a quiet time sharing a book with him.

In this chapter we have focused on cultivating creativity in toddlers:

* showing genuine interest
* getting down low to communicate with them
* giving them eye contact
* talking to them, but respecting their personal space
* showing them how to do things when they are stuck
* protecting them from being overwhelmed by their older sibling when necessary
* recognising that pretending is energy-sapping
* providing a book to share when they have had enough
* having a cuddle
* being sensitive to their interests and moods.

Reflective questions

Toddlers engage in 'literal' play and are on the verge of 'pretend' play, which is beginning to emerge. Play with a toddler and encourage them to pretend they are drinking, paying for something in a shop, driving a car, etc. Follow the child's lead to see what interests them and build on that interest.

Useful texts

Bruce, T. (2011) *Learning Through Play: Babies, Toddlers and the Foundation Years.* Hodder Education: London.

Bruce, T., Meggitt, C. And Grenier, J. (2010) *Child Care and Education, 5th Edition.* Hodder Education: London.

Manning Morton, J. And Thorp, M. (2003) *Key Times for Play.* Open University Press: Maidenhead.

8 How adults can help creative ideas to be cultivated

Creativity doesn't come from nowhere

So far in this book we have dwelt on the importance of offering a rich range of material provision which will give children plentiful experiences that they may then use as the germ of a creative idea. Some of these creative thoughts may then develop, by means of what is called creative processing, into an idea that is expressed overtly. This is called a creation. Again, having a wide range of material provision is of great importance because we are all so different in our modes of taking creative ideas to fruition. Some like to dance their ideas, some to make them into musical expressions. Some form scientific theories, or mathematical patterns, while others write poems and stories, make drawings, paintings, collages and sculptures and pottery.

We need to remember that babies, toddlers and young children have not yet lived for very long. They need to be offered direct and real experiences because, as we saw earlier in the book, creativity doesn't come from nowhere. It feeds off our experiences. It depends on experience of life in order for creative ideas to develop.

Figure 8.1 The girl is making a road. She has experience of roads in real life. Children use their real experiences in their creative play.

Figure 8.2   Although she is deeply engaged in her play,
this girl likes the companionship of the
adult who is nearby

Figure 8.3   She places the car in the gap. It fits exactly.
She is gathering ideas as she plays. Some
will take root and be developd, others will
not. This is all part of the creative process.

We also need to remember that we will probably see more creative ideas developing (the process of creating) than actually come to fruition to become acts of creation (the product or creation). In this respect, children and adults are rather similar. However, we are all helped to be more creative, both in the ideas we have and in the likelihood that our creative ideas will become externalised into creations, if other people support and encourage our creative thinking.

Margaret Donaldson (1992: 256), in her book *Human Minds*, emphasises the importance of adults in children's learning. She warns against extreme approaches, saying children need to spend time with adults who 'avoid being bound to a single point of view'. Those who are what she calls extremely child-centred, or perhaps extremely culture-centred, disadvantage children in different ways:

> If education is culture-centred, then conformity, decorum and the conveying of information are overvalued, and there is an underestimation of the child's ingenuity, imagination and initiative. There is also an underestimation of the human capacity for defiance and rejection and of the dire effects of boredom.
>
> ... the main risk of the child-centred extreme is that of overestimating children's powers of self-direction and the validity of their judgements, while underestimating not only their need for systematic, well-thought-out help but also their willingness to receive this help if it is not forced upon them in insensitive ways.

(Donaldson, 1992: 256–257)

Figures 8.4–8.5 The practitioner and the child play together with the hoop. They talk about the techniques of doing this together, and this helps the skill to develop.

Cultivating creativity

* The provision of experiences which feed creative ideas.
* Being offered a wide range of materials through which to express creative ideas.
* Being helped to learn the skills and techniques that are needed in order to use a particular medium or material on a 'need to' basis.
* Organising a learning environment which provokes, in many ways, the 'need to' learn skills and techniques useful for lifelong creativity.
* Being given the time and personal space, as well as the discussions and respectful help where needed, to develop an interest.
* Being helped in the way that is needed at that moment to develop an interest.

Children learn more and with deeper quality if they find things that interest them. This is not therefore a sentimental or romantic view of learning, it actually maximises the most effective ways of learning.

The provision of experiences and materials which feed into creative ideas and processes

As the learning gets under way in the homes and group settings in this book, there is a great emphasis on the experiences the children are offered and helped to get the most from by identifying and cultivating their interests.

Because children are free to be selective, make choices and come to decisions, they become very focused. Deep concentration cultivates creativity. Creativity takes a great deal of intense energy. This is not the kind of concentration where the adult sets the child a task and the child attends to it; this is the sort of concentration initiated by the child.

Figure 8.6   These boys are using the trucks in an unusual, unconventional and creative way. They have made them into tables.

Children are to be found in all corners and areas of the indoor and outdoor learning environment if the learning is rich. For some choices they often need adult support, such as cooking, sewing and woodwork. Perhaps because the techniques are particularly challenging for physical and mental coordination when learning to cook or sew, we see less creativity here. However, children often have creative ideas about sewing, woodwork and cooking, so, if adults were on the lookout for them, they could help the children to develop these ideas into creations. There is a tendency to insist on the result of the cooking or sewing looking like a perfect product, but sometimes a less perfect result may have involved the child in more creative thinking.

Sharing a book with an adult is an area of provision where there is an emphasis on telling and retelling a story. However, here again children will often introduce their own creative thoughts around the text. This is why sharing stories one to one or in very small groups, where there can be plenty of discussion and encouragement of the children's ideas, cultivates creativity.

Figure 8.7   The boys tell the story of the monsters, which has been part of their play, and the practitioner writes it down (scribes). In the next chapter we see the play scenario they created and how that came about. Here we see them telling the story after the play has finished. Sometimes, and only if the children are enthusiastic to do so, the scribed story will be kept and put in the book corner, perhaps with photographs and drawings so that it can be enjoyed further.

Figure 8.8   The boys bring the dinosaur book to the practitioner to help her understand what they are telling her and to give more insight into their play scenario. They concentrate intensely. Boys often enjoy this kind of introduction to literacy, especially when it is out of doors and action packed. It often encourages them to have a go at writing.

Figure 8.9   Seeing adults write encourages children to do so.

Figure 8.10 The boys share the book with the practitioner. One boy writes on the clipboard.

There are other areas of provision where adults have traditionally had expectations that the children will have their own creative ideas. The workshop area is one of these. The sandpit, wooden block play and small world are others.

As we have seen in the play scenario of the boys hunting monsters, it is easier to explain something after you have created it than it is before you make it. They would have found it very difficult to become involved in the scribing before the play had taken place. It can be damaging to the idea to try to pin it down into concrete words before it has been developed and turned into a creation. We often don't know exactly what we are trying to create until we have created it (Gura, 1992). This is as true for creative adults as it is for children. For example, a child will develop ideas about what they are creating as they make contact with the wooden blocks. It is difficult to envisage the finished construction of blocks in advance – it is too abstract. This is because the ideas begin to take a more tangible form as they work with the blocks, or in creating a pretend play scenario about hunting monsters. When we look at how scientists and artists create, we see that the processes which lead to creative products are necessarily fluid and, like play, need to remain in a state of flow (Bruce, 1991) and not be set in concrete when they only half-exist at that stage of creativity.

Figures 8.11–8.12   The boy is experimenting with using the hand and then the spoon to see if the results are the same in the orange paint sludge. These are variations on the theme of mark-making in the sludge, initiated here by this toddler.

Variations on a theme

Finding out and experimenting with doing the same thing in different ways are an aspect of creative processes. Making new connections which arise out of old ideas and habits is part of creativity. It is as if the child is asking, 'Will the result always be the same?' For example:

* Does jumping always cause a splash?

* Does jumping in different ways change the splash?

> Two strategies for exploring and developing creative ideas
>
> * Variation on a theme.
>
> * Keep doing the same thing.

Varying a theme, and repeating the same thing over and over again, are aspects of schemas. A schema (Athey, 1990) is a pattern of behaviour which can be repeated, generalised and used in different situations. A child who consistently uses lines (trajectories), going back and forth across the bridge in different ways (horizontal trajectories), but also jumping in a line up and down (vertical trajectories) as well as going from side to side towards, into and away from the puddle, has a trajectory schema.

In the last chapter, we shall see that the composer J.S. Bach used one theme and musical key and varied this in 18 different pieces of music (fugues) grouped together in a book called *The Art of the Fugue*. This is more than the everyday creativity we see most of the time. This is world-shaking creativity, which is very rare.

Being offered a wide range of materials through which to develop and express creative ideas

As they select from the experiences they are offered, the children begin to have ideas, some of which show the hallmarks of being creative ideas. The important thing is that the children are given opportunities to make choices and decisions, and that they are given sustained periods of time in which to develop their ideas.

The children are not having world-shaking creative thoughts but they are nevertheless having creative ideas as they try things out, rearrange what they know and expect, and explore consistencies and variations. Everyday creativity is as exciting for the person involved as world-shaking creativity is for the world! Because the environment provokes learning and cultivates it, the children are encouraged in their creativity. This is hugely because of the way the adults work with the children. It is also because of the way the experiences and material provision are organised, presented and used with the children.

The learning environment will hopefully be a well-thought-through learning environment, both indoors and outdoors. But it is of fundamental importance to remember to 'seize the moment' when working with children. Things happen quite unexpectedly, spontaneously and in completely unplanned ways. When a moth lands on a child's jacket in the garden, this is a golden opportunity to stop, look, wonder and discuss. Adults might, when it is over and the moth has flown away, and the moment has passed, go to find a book about moths in the bookcase. They could then look at this later with the children involved, or show it to the group when reporting exciting things that happened that day. This is why a good book resource is essential to a productive learning environment. Spontaneous, unplanned events often form the beginning of a creative idea in a child. Creativity is hugely about making new connections, and rearranging what is already known.

Figures 8.13–8.16   The boy has sufficient control and skill to be able to jump and make patterns of splash as he jumps. He can control the medium in which he is working. The influence of street dancing can be seen in his style, which is creative.

Freedom with guidance

Some skills are acquired through practice and having a go, but many need to be taught. Friedrich Froebel, the pioneer of education whose influence remains today in deep and far-reaching ways, saw the importance of helping children to develop skills in ways which hold meaning for them. The child in the photograph who can perform dance-like movements and control the water in a puddle feels competent, has control (autonomy), is creative and is confident.

In the photograph below, a boy is having a go at pouring himself a drink of water. He overfills the tumbler, but he knows how to mop up the spillage and he gets it right the next time and drinks with a feeling of success and pleasure. A short conversation with the practitioner has helped him to focus on the top of the tumbler as he fills it and to stop pouring the water before it reaches the top. He achieves this and is very pleased with himself for being so skilful. This is evident in the look of pleasure in the photograph as he drinks from the tumbler. But he needed the adult's help in developing this skill, and he may need to be reminded of this the next time he pours a drink until the skill is established and embedded.

Figure 8.17 The boy decides to pour himself a drink of water.

This is not the child's idea – it is the adult's idea. This again has nothing to do with the child developing creativity out of their own experience. Neither has the child hatched the idea and made it into a sculpture or wall relief. The adult has in effect used the child's drawing and turned it into their own agenda.

In this kind of adult-led activity, the child's creative ideas are not developed. Instead, there is a very public celebration of the adult's ideas, presented as if they are the child's ideas. This undermines the creative ideas that are in the child at the time, and it also has implications for the child's future development. It does not cultivate the child's creativity. It shows no interest in the child's ideas. It only encourages children to participate in the adult's creative agenda. It misleads adults into thinking they are encouraging creativity in children.

Adults who join the play with sensitivity

Something that has a powerful influence on children's creativity is what happens when an adult sits and joins the play as it flows along by:

* joining the child;
* tuning in by using skilled participative observation;
* finding the child's creative idea;
* helping the child to develop it;
* avoiding imposing their ideas and so taking over the child's idea;
* enjoying seeing the child's idea come to fruition in the creation of a story.

Being helped in the right way at the right time

Adults have to make decisions on the spot as they support creativity in action. The adult needs to support the child's creative ideas (the process of creativity) but to support the child in bringing the creative idea to fruition (creative product). Children need the right help in the right way at the right time.

The help needed at the woodwork bench is of a different kind from the help needed as a child becomes a dance maker (Davies, 2003: 158). As we saw in an earlier chapter, it is often difficult to distinguish between making and performing dances, especially for young children, 'whose dance is dancing and dancing is the dance'.

Mollie Davies points out that dance creativity in young children 'needs to take place within a broad framework which can be adapted as situations demand'. As adults helping children to create dances of their own, we need to address some questions she raises.

* What are the structuring devices for making a dance?
* Do they facilitate or restrict the children?
* How should we use the structuring devices with a particular child?
* Should we use structuring devices at all with young children?

She points out that the first dances young children make tend to be full of contrast: 'at one time gentle and calm, at another fierce and stormy, for example, as it sweeps through the space, makes a bid for the sky and literally collides with the earth'.

Because, as she points out, three- and four-year-olds typically move from one thing to another as they dance, they allow the 'different threads of their dancing to emerge and intertwine'. There is no point or benefit in offering structuring devices to children too early, as they need plenty of time for what Davies calls 'exploratory dance-play', such as children dancing in their ballet outfits, or being clowns.

However, as Sybil Marshall (1963) points out, we need to know enough about the subject to know and understand what the children need to know about making a dance. Davies says we need to introduce them in the right way at the right time to what she calls dance 'architecture'. This is what Donaldson emphasised at the beginning of this chapter. Children need our help in learning the culture, whether it is dance, music, mathematics, science, the visual arts, literature or drama. We need to encourage their ingenuity and creativity, giving them the 'basics' in the way Langer (1997) suggests, by helping them to make the basics fit them as individuals, rather than requiring them to fit the cultural norms, boringly and in a commonplace way.

Helping children to be creative learners in the visual arts

John Matthews (2003) points out that self-initiated and self-directed learning in every area is important for babies, toddlers and young children. However, he also stresses the key role of adults in cultivating the creativity of children. He focuses on the way this develops in the visual arts. He uses the metaphor of a developmental landscape with:

> many crossroads at which children must choose a direction. Although children sometimes appear to get stuck in apparent impasses, these hold-ups need not be permanent.
>
> (Matthews, 2003: 196)

If we observe the children, using our knowledge of how children develop, and alongside this keep learning about the visual arts, we will find that children show us in their 'action, play and media use' (Matthews, 2003: 196), as well as in words or signs, what they are interested in. We can then give them what they need in ways which help them through an impasse.

Strategies (arising from the work of Matthews (2003: 200) with children in the UK and in Singapore) which help children through an impasse are shown in the box below.

Helping children through an impasse in creative learning

* When children are frustrated, help them by encouraging them to search the environment for an image or example they want.

* They may find it helpful to look at a photograph, or image of another artist, to see how three dimensions can be translated into two dimensions.

* Looking at how someone else has done something and using it in your own drawing or painting is not 'copy painting' if it helps you to carry out your idea.

* Help children to use people who are more experienced than them to show examples of how something can be technically drawn or joined to make a model. Teaching a skill when it is needed is very helpful to children as they develop their creativity.

* Be genuinely interested in what the children have drawn, painted or made. They are then likely to want to discuss the techniques and content more readily than if you focus only on what interests you.

* When children share their drawings, paintings and models with you, they are not wanting you to offer a critique ('Where are the teeth?'). They want you to say which bits are interesting ('I like the way you have shaded there. What were you thinking?').

* Don't draw or paint for children. Draw for yourself, at your own level, and join in when they draw, so that they see adults drawing and painting as part of everyday living. Talk about the techniques and technical problems as you go.

* Make sure that showing them you as a sketcher, painter, sculptor is only a small part in a larger approach of your interest in their creativity in the visual arts.

Each of these bullets has been related to the visual arts, but they could just as well be used to help children cultivate their creative learning in the humanities, sciences or other arts (dance, music, drama, literature). Help with making dances, in the right way, at the right time.

Because transition from one idea to the next is an important aspect of making a dance, Davies (2003: 159) suggests that we can be very helpful if we give children experience of opposites, such as 'quick and slow'. Just commenting, 'I noticed you went quick and then very slow' is often enough to bring awareness to the child, and then they can repeat the dance they have made (choreographed) again and again, for family and friends.

Giving children the technical know-how

Every subject has its technical know-how. Sybil Marshall, headteacher of a rural primary school, was an English literature specialist and gave her children the structural devices needed to write creatively. In order to be able to offer children technical know-how in a variety of subjects, practitioners working with young children need to be as highly educated and well trained as possible, and to see themselves on a learning journey.

Just as poetry needs words and sculpture requires substances such as clay or wood, so dance composition needs movement. As children become more and more familiar with the language of dance – the material of movement – they slowly begin to differentiate between the process and the product. Unless they achieve familiarity with a wide range of movement expression, creativity cannot effectively take place. Instead, children will be seen to produce the same movements and movement patterns time and time again (Davies, 2003: 161).

We keep coming back to the importance of the adult role in cultivating creativity in young children.

In this chapter we have explored the role of the adult in helping children to be creative learners.

* Give children wide-ranging, broad, rich experiences which offer them choice, opportunities to experiment and find out how materials function
* Be interested in what the child is interested in and don't try to make them change to what you are interested in
* Give them sensitive help to follow through their interest by giving them what they need in order to do this
* Be a good observer and study both child development and subjects (dance, science, etc.) so that you develop the technical know-how of the subject and also spot the right moment to offer structural devices to the child
* When you teach, directly, a skill or technique, don't expect that 'one size fits all'. Remember that you need to help the child make a basic technique fit them as an individual. They need to use the basics (the tennis stroke, the handwriting techniques, woodwork, dance, making a story) to suit them as a unique person
* As you help them, give them the techniques and structural devices which will help them to think and be aware of their own learning.

Reflective questions

What are the essential skills of dance, drawing, wooden block play? How can you offer children open-ended experiences and give them the help they need to develop their technical know-how and feel free to try out their ideas?

Useful texts

Bruce, T. (2004) *Developing Learning in Early Childhood*. Paul Chapman Publishing: London.

Bruce, T. (2011) *Early Childhood Education, 4th Edition*. Hodder Education: London.

Davies, M. (2003) *Movement and Dance in Early Childhood, 2nd Edition*. Paul Chapman Publishing: London.

Matthews, J. (2003) *Drawing and Painting: Children and Visual Representation, 2nd Edition*. Paul Chapman Publishing: London.

9 Creations

The focus of this book is on cultivating creativity. Creativity has these aspects:

* emergent beginnings;
* the process of developing a creative thought or idea (being creative);
* the product which emerges (being a creator).

It is not possible to have a creative product without it being the result of the creative processes that led to it.

It is possible to develop creative ideas and thoughts which do not emerge and become creative products.

We need to understand the different needs of children as they are involved in the different aspects of creativity. We need to offer the right help at the right time in the right way if we are to cultivate their creativity. We need to give them the opportunities and time to explore, select and meander and find ideas which they may not consciously know they have. We need to structure the environment indoors and out of doors so that it is conducive to the cultivation of creativity.

Figure 9.1 The boy wants to make a mask as part of the costume he has in his mind for hunting monsters. He begins with the mask, because this is a familiar prop which he has some experience of making previously. After that, he makes the spear, the shield and the helmet.

Figure 9.2   He needs some help and asks the practitioner to put the eyes in the correct place. He has made masks for his pretend-play scenarios before and so knows what he wants. But he does not say he wants a mask. The adult guesses this and responds by helping him, but also saying, 'Let me help you make your mask. Where do you want the eyes?'

Figure 9.3   His friend imitates the mask-making and manages to make one by himself. Children learn a huge amount from observing each other, as well as learning from the adults who help them.

Having creative intentions

Piaget would say the boy had an intention he could not articulate in words and appreciated the adult recognising this.

Bruner would argue that the adult has tuned into the child's incipient intention by talking 'as if' that is what the child had in mind.

Vygotsky would say that the boy made this mask-like shape incidentally and that it was only because the adult commented on it that he became aware of it (Vila, 1996).

The development of **intention** is important but, where creativity is concerned, it is often best left as a very flexible thing. This means that children should not be expected to put their intentions into words in advance of what they make or as they are developing an idea. The intention really just needs to be a rough line of a general direction, so that the child can be the one who forms the idea and the adult doesn't snatch a half-forming idea from them and turn it into their own adult creation. When intention changes from being the child's developing and still-forming creative idea to being the adult's fully formed idea, creativity in the child is destroyed rather than cultivated. This was something that emerged as an important issue when adults worked with children in the Froebel Blockplay Research Project (Gura, 1992: 23) at the Froebel Institute in the 1990s. But it is helpful to children if adults articulate what is happening as it unfolds. In this case, the adult is talking about mask-making during the process of making masks for the characters in the monster hunt.

Adults helping children to make things in the workshop area need to bear in mind:

* problems arise when children are asked to verbalise in advance of action;
* lack of pressure for the child to speak is important;
* language without action decontextualises situations;
* adults can be helpful by talking about what is happening;
* formal advance planning constrains the imagination and discourages flexible thinking;
* other strategies from the adult may help children to think more effectively in advance about what to do.

A three-year-old girl found a caterpillar in the garden. She arrived next day with a toy caterpillar and decided to make one out of blocks. Then she chose to draw the block model of her toy caterpillar. She found she had added an extra leg on one side. The next day she reconstructed her block model, using the sketch to guide her. She remembered to deduct the extra leg!

(Gura, 1992: 23)

We can see from this example that helpful adults have cultivated the girl's creative intentions in ways which are right for her, and with very good results. She has been able to think creatively over time and to make a product which can be reconstructed to look exactly the same again and again.

The desire to get the creation exactly as you want it!

Often, children at about the age of four years become very fascinated by making functional creations. For example, a child might make an aeroplane, using a well-tried method, and this becomes a formula for making aeroplanes. But being able to repeat a formula over and over again is not creative. It will be important that the child varies and innovates around the model aeroplane designs or he will not be a creative learner. The time is now right for him to learn more about the aerodynamics of flight. This is where staff need to learn, too. Just as in dance, children need to learn the structural devices of how to transition and link one dance idea to the next, so in engineering and science they need to know about wing and body shapes which allow lift-off. Children depend on adults to help them in this.

Figures 9.4–9.7   Making a helmet proves to be quite a challenge. The joy of thinking he has managed it is dashed as he puts it on, and he is overwhelmed with disappointment. He needs the help of the practitioner to carry through his idea.

Figure 9.8   His friend manages to make a helmet which, although less elaborate, pleases him as it is comfortable to wear, which satisfies him.

Of course, we do need to be careful because sometimes children are happy if their creation is purely an image that suggests a likeness to something. They don't want it to be functional. The model 'suggests' aeroplane, and that is enough. But for other children, they want their aeroplane to fly. In the monster-hunt scenario, the boys definitely wanted their play props, which they created, to be functional. They wanted to use them in the play. But children can quickly become frustrated and give up when it proves challenging to turn their idea into what they want.

Creative process is about creating resources and ideas to be used later

Children often seem to show no interest in keeping the paintings, drawings or models that they make. This is because these are part of the creative process, rather than coming to fruition as a product. Finger-painting experiences are not usually about creative products. They give children the opportunity to discover, experience, meander, drift, identify thoughts and ideas, and see how they form. This kind of experience is not about making a creative product.

Some children love to make drawings to enable their ideas to flow, but when they do, they are unlikely to be bothered about keeping the drawing or seeing it displayed. It is important to ask children whether they want a drawing or painting displayed before putting it on a wall. It may have been part of the creative process and not thought of as a definite creation.

One of Matthew's first words was 'digger'. He was fascinated by diggers as a toddler and would gaze at diggers he saw at road works. His favourite toy was a digger. It is hardly surprising that one of his first major drawings was of a digger, when he was four years old. It was drawn on scrap paper. He gave it to his grandparents, because he was at their house when he drew it. It was a creation, but it emerged out of the processes of his creative learning.

Kit (four years old) also enjoyed drawing at his grandparents' house. His grandfather wrote on the back of one of his drawings:

> Having drawn the black parts Kit kept on about something 'sticking out'. Only when he drew the blue water and the diver did we realise that he meant the famous Tudor ship, the *Mary Rose*.

He had watched a television programme with his grandparents about the lifting of the Tudor ship, the *Mary Rose*. A few days later he visited them again. They had left a newspaper cutting about this event on a coffee table. He must have noticed this and he used the idea in his spontaneous drawing on a piece of scrap paper.

The same is true of play scenarios in that they, too, are about process more than product. Free-flow play (Bruce, 1991) is not meant to be captured and pinned down into a creative product. It becomes a reservoir of experiences to be called on for storytelling, poetry making, in literature and drama.

The child who spends hours at the woodwork bench trying things out, varying how they do things, using different materials and tools, is making a future store to be drawn upon. It is a bit like squirrels storing nuts and forgetting where they bury them, then finding them later when they are needed. We sometimes say that children are busy doing nothing. The 'nothing' is crucial as part of creative learning. Children often need to meander and find their direction before they have a clear idea of what they want to do or make. They need time and personal space to identify ideas, select, experiment, vary an action or material, gather ideas, and have the kind of concentration that goes with deep thinking. This kind of creative learning is often discouraged by adults who don't understand the kind of learning that does not look 'purposeful'.

Creative ideas grab children as they develop their play scenarios

Play is about process and not about keeping products.

Children who have only a narrow range of choice (or no choice at all if they are required to fulfil adult-led activities all day) cannot develop their creative ideas using the medium they are most comfortable in. After all, some of us love to dance. Some of us love to paint. Some of us love to make mathematical thoughts and solutions. We all have our preferred media and, if we are allowed to use our strengths, we can learn more deeply and be more creative (flexible and mobile in our thoughts). In the following photographs, the two boys favour pretend play as their medium. They are creating a monster hunt.

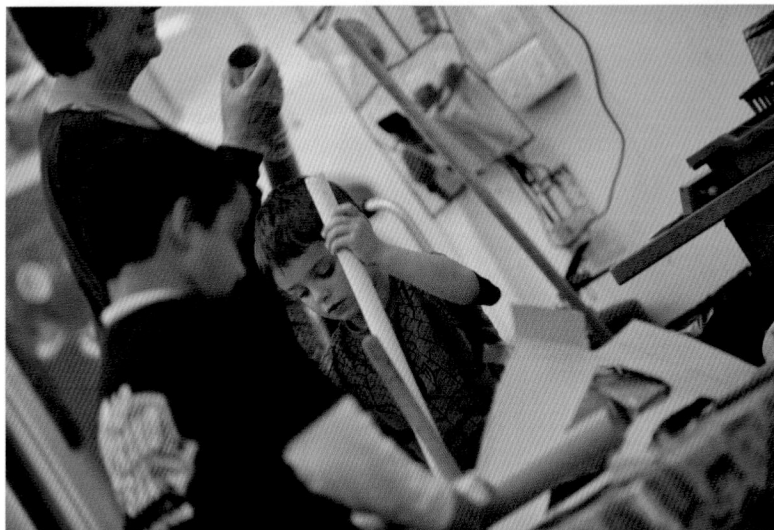

Figure 9.9   The boys select tubes ready to turn them into spears to hunt the monsters. The practitioner goes to find some more.

Figure 9.10   They show the practitioner the chart of dinosaurs and explain that these are like the monsters they will hunt with the spears they are making.

Figures 9.11–9.12 They spend some time discussing with considerable excitement and energy how to make the tip of the spear. The practitioner offers the suggestion of cutting up egg boxes, and they take over, taping them onto the spear. These are both children with English as an additional language. They rely on the practitioner to give them the vocabulary they need, such as spear and tip. Younger children watch and gather ideas, storing them away for the future.

Dens as creations

Another example of a finished creation is Tom's 'A' house, which he made in the garden when he was seven years old. Sometimes we can see glimmerings of earlier creative influences on a creation. We keep saying throughout this book that, more often than not, we can't tell how a creative idea began. The phase of gradually identifying an idea and gathering thoughts around it usually remains hidden to us. But here we can see that Tom, from the age of about three years, has been using a woodwork bench. He has learned to join pieces of wood with a hammer and to use a vice. He has been making criss-cross aeroplane configurations since then.

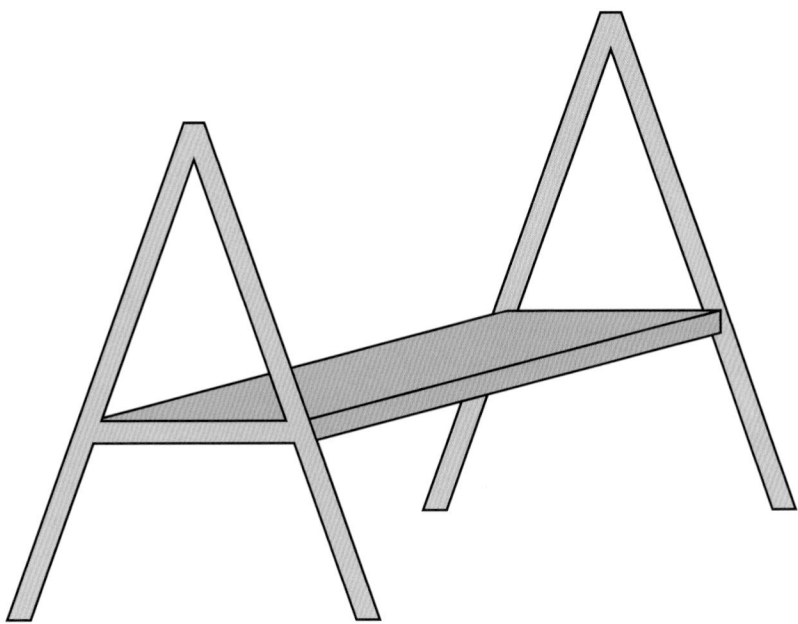

Figure 9.13   The 'A' house.

Recently at school the teacher took the children in Tom's class for a mathematical walk as part of a project on triangles and other shapes. She showed the children how triangles are used to strengthen buildings.

A little while after the project, Tom was playing in the garden with a friend and they wanted to build a den. As Helen Tovey (2007) says, all over the world children build dens as part of their play. Tom and his friend Ben were typical in this. As the day went on, they used their knowledge of triangles and, with a hammer, nails and wood, made an 'A' house, as they called it. They wanted to sleep on the platform, hanging blankets over the apex to make a tent-like construction. They were allowed to do so, and Tom's mother slept nearby in the garden so that they could be safe.

Here we can see the creative learning (process) and how it led to a creation (the 'A' house).

* **Prepare/gather thoughts** – unconsciously identifying a vague thought that lingers.
* **Simmer the thoughts** – gathering thoughts around it, without realising this.
* **Illuminate and clarify** – being obviously interested in it and becoming aware of this.
* **Hatching** – trying to make ideas more formed and tangible.
* **Hatched** – a creation emerges.

A completely different example would be Hannah (seven years old) and her friend Anna (six years old), who made a café. They spent days setting up everything they would need. They begged plastic cutlery from adults, borrowed crockery, made a cash register, invoices, cheque books, and cooked biscuits. They made fresh orange juice, using a recipe. They both attended the cookery club every Wednesday afternoon during school time. They made menus and table cloths from old sheets which they were allowed to decorate using felt pens. They made waitress hats out of folded paper. They had learned all these techniques at one time or another at school.

For several days they were involved in 'free-flow play' (Bruce, 1991, 2011a, 2011b), using dolls and various friends to develop the play scenario. John Matthews (2003) notes the importance of children having opportunities to flow across several days in their play, especially at this age.

The play scenario turned into a creation when they asked if they could invite neighbours to 'really have tea' in their café, and if they could raise funds for the *BBC Television Children in Need* appeal. They did both, so the 'free-flow play' became a creation which was pinned down and took a definite lasting shape. This was now a café, rather than children playing cafés. They moved from being creative to being creators.

Figures 9.14–9.15 Once the play props are made, the challenge then becomes making best use of them and incorporating them into the character and the story line. How do you keep a mask on when you are holding your spear? It is fun to practise falling and moving as a rehearsal, before the play begins to flow. Children often limber up, so to speak, before they launch into free-flow play.

Figure 9.16   Is it possible to move as freely as the character needs in the costume made?

Figure 9.17   At transitional moments (from making the props to going outside for the play scenario) children often need the help of an adult or older child.

Figures 9.18–9.19 Feeling supported in their play scenario, the boys begin to flow in their play, but they still appreciate having the practitioner with them, and they tell her what is happening as they go. It is as if they are making an improvised script as they play.

Play scenarios are a powerful resource of ideas for later use

Children, typically from about four years of age, may be happy to tell their play scenarios to an adult, as Vivian Gussin Paley (1984) has experienced. They may be happy to dictate them for the adult to scribe and to act them out with friends later at circle time. This is by no means always the case, and Gussin Paley works with great sensitivity with the children on this. Children can go to a specially designated table and dictate their story if they wish, but are under no pressure to do so.

> Boys narrate superhero adventures filled with dangerous monsters, while girls place sisters and brothers, mothers and fathers in relatively safe roles. If lost, they are quickly found, if harmed they are healed or replaced. Boys tell of animals who kill or are killed; girls seldom involve animals in violence. A bear or lion encountered in the forest is likely to lead a girl home and will not be shot and eaten for supper.
>
> (Gussin Paley, 1984: 204)

In this way, children begin to see how play scenario ideas can be used to create stories which become written down, to become dramas that can be performed again and again. In the last chapter, we focused on this aspect and saw how the monster-hunt scenario was scribed, to be kept and used again and again. The free-flow play (Bruce, 1991), which is about the process of creativity, then changes into a creation, something to be kept and used again and revisited.

For every time we become aware of the creative thinking that a child is involved in, there are probably many more creative thoughts that we never come to know about.

We can tune into someone else's creative idea and appreciate their creation by:
* doing the same thing and using the person's idea;
* talking about what is happening;
* rephrasing what the other person says, putting it into our own words;
* making parallel remarks: 'I've made an enclosure just like yours. Now I'm going to put a lorry in it, like you did.'

The volcano

Children love nooks and crannies as well as wide-open spaces in which to run about. Creative ideas often develop in hidden-away places off the beaten path. The entrance hall, where an adult greets families on arrival and stays on to chat to children, is a good example of this.

When children know there will be an adult interested in helping them to develop their deepest thoughts, they find their way to that spot with regularity. On this particular morning, two boys decide to make a volcano. They find a cloth and place scraps of paper on it to represent the lava. The adult, as if by magic, has a book about volcanoes. This is a crucial element in the creative process. Because there is a great emphasis on building a good fiction and non-fiction library, books on every subject can be produced in seconds. Staff know the library they have developed inside out, and distribute the books around the building according to the children's interests and needs.

Girls begin to join the volcano building. There is plenty of discussion about volcanoes along the way. This is another very important point. This really is discussion, rather than the adult telling the children about volcanoes. Children's scientific stories are listened to and built on.

One of the boys thinks that the orange Play-Doh™ in the main room would be just right for the lava. The adult encourages him to fetch some, suggesting he should tell an adult in the room why he needs it. This is another important aspect of the way adults work with the children. There is a team commitment to cultivating creativity in the children. This means that strict adherence to narrowly followed rules is not the order of the day. Instead there are clear and firm boundaries which the children help to make, so that the environment is safe and equipment is not damaged. Whether dough can be removed is open to negotiation as situations arise.

The children know that they will need to discuss any changes to the usual boundaries. Once the temporary change in boundary can be seen to be official, and because the orange dough is carefully placed on the volcano, other children begin to bring Play-Doh™. We see them imitating and using the 'side-by-side' strategy as they place their 'lava' alongside the boy's to run down the slopes of the volcano.

At the end of the morning, the volcano is left as a creation in the entrance hall for others to appreciate. The intensity and depth of creative thinking that developed (the process) were an important reason why the volcano became a creation (product). We can see that being creative thinkers led the children into becoming creators – of a volcano.

Penny Holland (2003) suggests that adults need to be more sensitive to the needs of boys in their dramatic play scenarios and to tune into their themes, even when they look as if they are going in directions of weapon play. Vivian Gussin Paley agrees that boys tackle themes of killing and death in their play scenarios more than girls. The volcano is violent. Children need to explore life and death scenes in their play, and at times will capture these in their creations.

In this chapter we have thought about creations resulting from creative thinking. The creations children make are very personal. They will share them only with those they trust and by whom they feel respected. There is nothing as deeply satisfying as sharing with a child the hatching out of a creative idea and finding that it has become a creation.

Reflective questions

Observe a group of children involved in a pretend-play scenario which they have initiated. How can you facilitate the play without taking it over and controlling it? Use some of the strategies in this chapter to help you support the children's play ideas, so that they get the most out of their play and maximise their creativity.

Useful texts

Gussin Paley, V. (1984) *Boys and Girls: Superheroes in the Doll Corner*. Chicago University Press: Chicago.

Holland, P. (2003) *We Don't Play with Guns Here: War, Weapons and Superhero Play in the Early Years*. Open University Press: Maidenhead, Philadelphia.

Hyder, T. (2005) *War, Conflict and Play*. Open University Press: Maidenhead.

Kalliala, M. (2005) *Play Culture in a Changing World*. Open University Press, McGraw-Hill: Maidenhead.

Everyday creativity, specialist creativity and world-shaking creativity

In this book, as we have seen in earlier chapters, the word 'creativity' is used as an umbrella term, with these three aspects under it:

1. spotting the signs of the emergent **beginnings of creativity**;
2. **being a creative learner**;
3. **making creations**.

We have looked at the beginnings of creativity in an earlier chapter, and throughout the book there has been an emphasis on the way that creative learning can be cultivated in young children. Sometimes, but not always, a creation emerges.

Everyday creative learners

For the most part, the creations of young children, whether they are from the visual arts, scientific theories, mathematical patterns and ideas, dances, musical improvisations or the creative way of relating to people and resolving conflicts and fairness issues, are of the everyday kind. This is not peculiar to children. It is the same for the majority of adults, too. Cooking a delicious meal, creative in its combination of ingredients, improvised from what is found in the fridge, cupboard and vegetable rack, is a much-appreciated kind of everyday creativity by those who share the meal with the cook.

Creativity in everyday life lifts living to levels of fulfilment, satisfaction, effective, deep and rigorous practical thinking which are in a different league to pedestrian, boring and commonplace living. Creativity makes life worth living, especially when the going is tough. It is linked with resilience and, in extreme cases, with survival. It means that we are using our intelligence to the full, flexibly, adaptively and imaginatively as we problem solve and generate new thoughts.

Being creative in everyday life is a good way of living. It develops a strong sense of self as a separate, autonomous person, with a sense of agency and control over what we can do to change things for the better. Being a creative learner also gives a sense of belonging and connectedness with others, and the knowledge that it is possible to contribute as well as take in life, and make things better not just for oneself but for others, too.

Most of this book is about cultivating everyday creative learning in young children, so that in their daily lives, throughout their lives, they will plan what they eat, cook, how they present their food, plan what they wear, arrange their homes, gardens, leisure interests and work and be creative as they do so. Some of us like to put our main emphasis on our leisure time and work, and not so much on daily shopping and home-making. Others are more focused on creative cooking, DIY, gardening and décor. Different people are creative in different ways – providing their creativity has been cultivated and not constrained or stamped out at an early stage or through lack of use.

Examples of creative approaches to living

* Making up a food recipe.
* Choosing your own design for a room (not copying an existing one).
* Redesigning your garden, using your own ideas.
* Drawing your own tapestry design and choosing the coloured threads to use.
* Making a cupboard with your own design.
* Making a dress or shirt by combining several paper patterns to fit your ideas of what you want.
* Planning a social gathering and carefully getting people together so that they enjoy it as much as possible.
* Planning a car route to take in scenery and good picnic spots suitable both for grandma, who has a Zimmer frame but loves to be in the countryside, and for a niece who is prone to hay fever.
* Making music and dance together with a large group at a party.

Specialist creative learners

There are many people who are highly expert in a particular area, who are completely unknown outside their field but who nevertheless are creative learners, finding deep satisfaction in the ideas they develop and bring to creation.

Looking at the childhood play of creative adults, artists, scientists and those involved in the humanities gives us some hints. Until recently there seemed to be only an associative link between smoking and cancer; through research, this has been recognised as a causal link. At the moment there are only glimpses of what might be associative links between childhood play and adult creativity.

Brain development and creativity

We are beginning to understand more about how the brain develops (Damasio, 1999). Children born into musical families hear music played from the beginning, and from an early age participate in music-making with their family. Studies reveal that these musicians have larger parts of the brain colonised for sound in the area that deals with language. This suggests that the more we use our brains to develop our creativity, the more we can be creative.

We don't know to what extent childhood play influences adult life, but it probably does have a lasting impact, which is used as a resource in later life. For example, the doll's house has been an important tradition in early childhood practice in the UK and other countries for a century or more. This kind of childhood play has probably impacted on the adult lives of many, but it has certainly influenced one adult artist, Katie Etheridge.

The visual arts

Katie is an installation artist. Her work is of great interest to those working with young children because it makes powerful links with her childhood experiences. In her work she uses the doll's house, her enjoyment of wearing dressing-up clothes and dancing, and the bones of a horse that she found as a child when on a family holiday in the New Forest. A film is projected onto the back wall of the large doll's house, featuring dancers dressed as the dolls who live in the house. They move from room to room as they dance. The staircase is made out of the spine of the horse's skeleton. Katie says of her installation, which is named *All That Remains*:

> Doll's houses, as miniature worlds created by children that they can control, relate back to the desire to make sense of the world.

Another part of her installation shows a video of a long-forgotten music hall dancer placed in a cabinet, which, she says:

> … invites thought on what is the sum of someone's life once they are gone, and how do they live on through the things they leave behind?

She continues:

> Collecting and sorting can be a way of trying to create order in a volatile and unpredictable universe. We turn our homes into miniature museums, choosing what to display and what to keep hidden away, inadvertently curating the remnants of our lives. Likewise, memories are ordered and filed by the unconscious mind. Some may lie buried deep and untouched for years. The objects we hold on to are historical artefacts in their own right, but also embody a deeper and entirely personal significance as triggers of memory. But what happens when we die and become relics ourselves?
>
> (Etheridge, 2001: 9)

We can see very clearly that her childhood experiences with a very happy family holiday, the loss of a loved person, her play with doll's houses and her enjoyment of dancing have all been part of the development of her ideas, which have resulted in a creation –*All That Remains*.

History

Our creative processes and the creations which emerge as a result revolve around people as well as objects, as we see in this work. The same may be said of Charlotte. She is an historian, studying the Cromwellian period. She takes part in historical re-enactments with a historical society. This involves making a costume that is historically accurate and reconstructing events of battles of that time. She has also constructed, with others, a character for herself, so that the re-enactment has some of the qualities of a drama improvisation. The framework is set by the historical facts, but history is also about people and how they experience events as unique individuals.

As a child, Charlotte spent many hours wearing dressing-up clothes and assuming different characters. Once again, we can see a resonance between her childhood play and her later creativity in the humanities.

Dance choreography

Hannah, on her fifth birthday, was given a cerise tutu. Her choreography changed, particularly as she had been very struck by seeing excerpts from *La Sylphide*. She spent a great deal of time trying to persuade her friend Wally to wear her kilt, like the male lead dancer in *La Sylphide*. She wanted him to lift her. He was not enthusiastic. Over the next few years she was continually frustrated in her desire to choreograph dances for others to perform. She was often clear what she wanted, and could obviously see dances in her head, but getting other children to perform them when they did not know how to dance the steps was a problem.

She found it easier to develop drama improvisations with her friends, and in her middle childhood there were several months when a prolonged play scenario took place in a dress shop, with a complaints department, accounts department and dress-making department, as well as fitting rooms and fashion shows.

It is as if 'a silent refrain from the future' is woven into a child's play, almost waiting for helpful adults to 'pick up the frequency' (Lively, 1993: 7). Adults who do 'pick up the frequency' can make a huge contribution to the future adult's creative development. It is these 'silent refrains from the future' which are fascinating when we observe young children such as Katie with her doll's house, Charlotte with her dressing-up clothes, Tom with his den building, Hannah with her dancing, Matthew with the mechanics of the digger or Kit with the beauty of the *Mary Rose*.

Hannah as an adult knows enough about the structure of different dance forms to make innovative, creative choreography of her own, blended with her knowledge of literary texts to make a very abstract dance based on Virginia Woolf's book *Moments of Being*. This is a long way from the little girl in the pink tutu, but the beginnings were there.

Resonances between childhood play and adult creativity

It is, of course, speculative to wonder if there could be any links between the childhood play and the adult creativity in these individuals' areas of specialism. As adults, Katie is an artist, Charlotte has a serious hobby in Cromwellian re-enactments, Tom is a cabinet maker, Matthew is a doctor, Kit reads philosophy and poetry in his leisure time, Hannah leads a mixed-media group in dance, drama, film and literary texts. We can ponder what the future creativity will be of a newly fledged walker, talker and pretender, putting dolls in and out of the doll's house, and many other children in this book. We can hope it will continue to be cultivated throughout their education as well as at home.

We know that doctors, dancers, writers, musicians, artists, historians, geographers, scientists, mathematicians develop the appropriate skills and technical know-how of their specialisms, but they need to do more than this if they are to be creative in their chosen subject of expertise. In order to go beyond commonplace knowledge of their specialism, they need to be able to use the basics of the subject flexibly. This means they use what they know intelligently and adaptively, and think of new ways of doing things, often because what they know doesn't quite work in a particular situation. We saw this in the example Ellen Langer gave when the basic technique they had been taught for playing tennis was varied and altered by tennis stars so that it would suit them as individuals.

When a doctor makes a diagnosis, it is not enough to know the basics. The basic knowledge has to be actively interpreted and thought about. This is how new medical techniques come about.

Creativity goes beyond the basics

Charlotte can do more than interpret Cromwellian re-enactments. She has, as an adult with an interest in the history of this period, developed a character for her Cromwellian self, complete with costume and artefacts, and is part of an imaginary Cromwellian family of characters, improvised with others during each re-enactment. This is a creative way of learning history. Re-enactments of scenes are not a new idea, but Charlotte brings new ideas to this through the character she has created. This is more than everyday creativity, because she has developed great depth of knowledge as she has gathered her ideas about this period of history. This means that she has become a specialist creator.

Scientific creativity

Sometimes we can clearly see how an everyday situation is looked at anew by a creative learner who has developed specialist knowledge. We are going to look at one of several creative contributions made by one scientist, to the study of crystals in chemistry. Here is the story of how this happened.

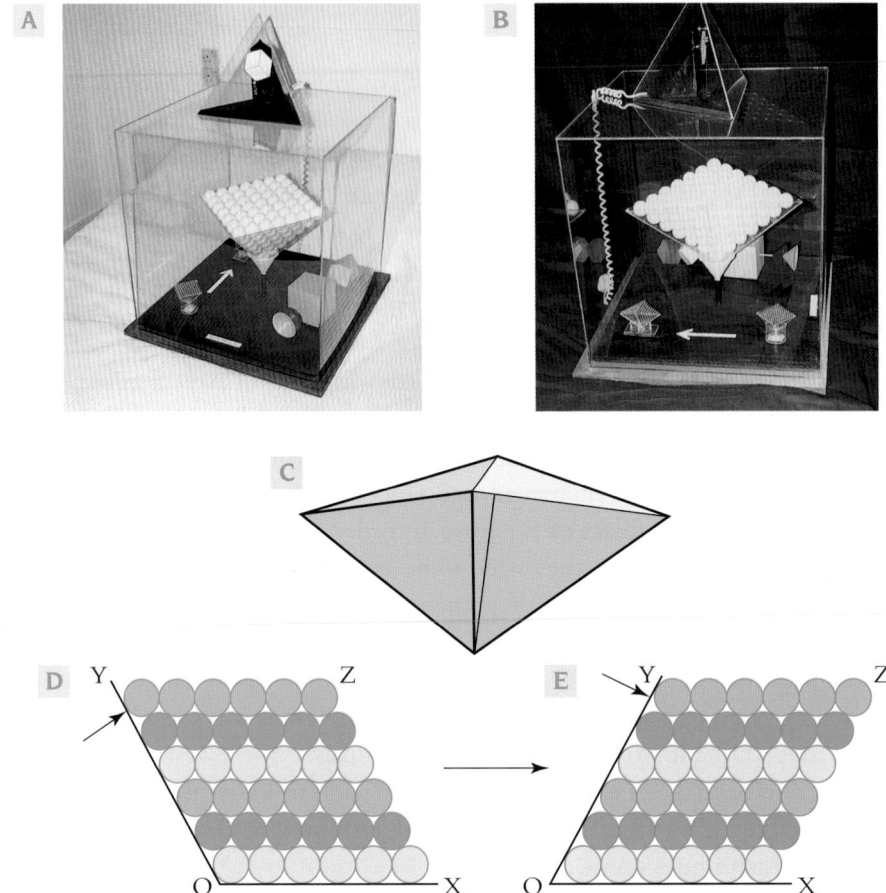

Figure 10.1 (A–E)

Crystals are part of our everyday lives

Few people realise just how important crystals are, yet they are part of our everyday lives. We wear them on our wrists or drive about in cars, trains and aeroplanes made of them, or use them to eat with, and many other things. This is because all metal objects are made from crystals, stuck together to form the components of watches, motor vehicles, knives, forks and so on. The reason that we are not aware of this is that they are usually so small that these tiny crystals can be seen only using powerful microscopes.

The crystals we do see in our everyday lives are those such as the sugar we crush in the bottom of a tea cup, or coarse salt we use in cooking. This helps us to see how crystals can be brittle and break up when we crush or grind them. It helps us to see why some things are brittle while some are not.

A scientist called Peter Rowland, an expert in the behaviour of metal, wanted to look at why we can bend metal wire without it crumbling to pieces, because metal wire is made up of brittle crystals. He decided a good way to do this would be to make models, using spheres to represent the atoms that make up the crystals in the metal wire.

In any crystal, the atoms are arranged in a regular pattern, like the three-dimensional bricks in a wall. To make a model of a crystal that contains enough atoms to be worth studying, he had to put together thousands of spheres in a regular three-dimensional pattern. It was a painstakingly long task.

He developed a creative way of doing this. He poured the spheres into a mathematically designed mould that ensured that they automatically lined up in the same way as would the crystals of a simple metal (like copper).

Photograph A shows a model of this crystal arrangement (which has since been made into a work of art, because crystal formations are very beautiful). Ping-pong balls have been used to represent the atoms in copper.

The interesting thing was that Peter Rowland found when the model was made in this way it could change form (deform) without the crystal structure breaking up. It wasn't brittle!

This can be seen in photograph B, where two diagonally opposite corners of the top surface have been pushed towards each other until the mould (and the crystal in it) has been transformed into two. To show this more clearly, Figure C shows the mould alone in its transformed state.

* One side is the blue pyramid with its top (apex) pointing to the right.
* One side is the pink pyramid with its tip pointing to the right.

These two pyramids are mirror images of each other, just as are the patterns of atoms inside them. They are called 'crystal twins'.

Squares, triangles and rotations – transformations!

Before the crystal structure transformed into the twin crystal pyramids, the top layer was a square pattern. It is as if the rotation made the two halves point in different directions and, in so doing, became two triangles.

The rotation came about because the layers of atoms in each half were sliding over each other in parallel directions. The direction was different for the stacks of atoms in the blue and pink pyramids. Figures D and E give some idea of how this happens.

The important thing is that the crystals can bend by the sliding of layers in this way. That is why a copper wire can bend. The crystals of sugar and salt can't bend in this way, so they are brittle and can be crushed and crumbled. Of course, it isn't quite as simple as that, but, as we are not expert scientists, this gives us enough understanding to see that the model which metallurgists named the 'Rowland Transformation', after the man who discovered it, helps scientists to know how transformations of this kind affect the strength, hardness and general properties of metals.

This is a good example of how something was staring mathematicians in the face for several thousand years before being spotted. It took a metallurgist, puzzling out how a piece of metal wire can bend, to see the structural connection with ancient geometrical constructions such as the pyramid-shaped piles of spherical stone missiles found in prehistoric forts, which are really upside-down versions of photograph A.

In this story of a scientist's journey we have seen how he was involved in the creative processes of:

* preparation;
* incubation;
* illumination;
* hatching

which resulted in a creative product: the Rowland Transformation model (1954–1955).

Literary creativity

Philip Pullman (2002), the writer, says there are three things he would like people who work with children to invoke, in order to cultivate a child's creativity:

1. Mystery
By mystery, I mean the delicate … trance-like business of letting a story come at you out of the shadows, without pestering it and jabbing questions at it like sticks.

2. Chance
By chance, I mean … experience of other things than educational … unpredictable catching fire that is most memorable.

3. Silence
By silence, I mean the freedom to … wander at will from one interesting thing to another, making no noise, drawn only by delight, and then to settle into the quiet and solitude of your own space and begin the long process of turning all you've gathered into honey.

The 'trance-like business' that Philip Pullman describes is rather like the period of preparation that is an important part of developing a creative idea that might be:

* scientific, like Peter Rowland's thoughts about grinding salt when we cook, mixed with vague thoughts about how the Egyptian pyramids were built and the bendiness of copper wire;
* of the humanities, like Nelson Mandela's Council of Reconciliation, which we shall look at next;
* artistic, like the dancer Isadora Duncan, whom we met at the beginning of the book, or the composer J.S. Bach, whom we shall meet at the end of the book.

The things that 'unpredictably catch fire' inside our minds and hearts and bodies are like the period of incubation as we develop our ideas, without realising we are doing so, but becoming aware that something exciting is going on inside us.

The way we are 'drawn by delight' about the interest we find in certain things leads to the illumination that comes with the development of a creative idea.

The 'honey' at the end of this process is the hatching out of a creation.

World-shaking creators

People who are world-shaking creators are rare. In this section of the chapter, we shall look at three. They come from different cultures and different historical times.

The humanities

The humanities deal with time, space and reasons for how people behave and structure their lives. The humanities include disciplines such as history, geography and the social sciences (e.g. psychology, anthropology and sociology).

Nelson Mandela, addressing the problem of acknowledging and acting on the way innocent people were tortured, murdered and terrorised during the period of apartheid in South Africa, created the Council of Reconciliation after he was elected president. This was an original idea of enormous implication because, for the first time in the history of that country, there was a spirit of reconciliation instead of a desire to punish through revenge, or through deterring others by public punishment and the humiliation of those who take part in the abuse of human rights. Punishment can be of three kinds:

1. revenge – an eye for an eye and a tooth for a tooth;
2. deterrent – putting people off committing a crime (e.g. a crime against humanity);
3. reform – helping people to admit what they have done, to see why it was wrong, and to do something about their future behaviour because they want to change and not because someone is forcing them to change.

The Nuremberg Trials after the Second World War were in the spirit of revenge and deterrence. The Council of Reconciliation set up by Nelson Mandela was a creative response to a challenge in the spirit of reform.

The sciences

The Polish astronomer Nicolas Copernicus (1473–1543) completed *De Revolutionibus* in 1530. He showed how the Earth rotated on its axis once daily, moving round the Sun once a year. This meant that the Earth was not the centre of the universe. This innovative and original theory changed the way scientists, and now most people, look at the stars and planets. It was called the Copernican Revolution. Because it was dangerous to suggest the Earth was not the centre of the universe, as the Christian Church regarded any threat to its doctrines as heresy to be punished by torture and death, Copernicus did not dare to publish his work and thus it was not published during his lifetime.

The arts

Interestingly, we cannot really talk about world-shaking creators in the arts, because everyone responds to dance, visual arts, literature and music in a very personal way. That is the whole point about them. That is the whole strength of the arts. Through the arts we can find creators who touch our hearts as well as our minds.

J.S. Bach (1685–1750), during the last year of his life, composed 18 fugues, published in a book called *The Art of the Fugue.*

* He used one theme.
* He always wrote in the form of music called a fugue.
* He wrote all 18 fugues in the same key of music.

But it really was an extreme case of variations on a theme. He made the pieces incredibly complex in the way that he varied the number of voices. In the penultimate fugue he inserted the letters of his name, BACH. This is called self-reference, and it has been suggested (Hofstadter, 2000: 86) that he was marking the closure of his life in this way, giving it a sense of completion. His son, Carl Philipp Emanuel (1750), wrote, 'I have let this final page of Bach's last fugue serve as an epitaph.'

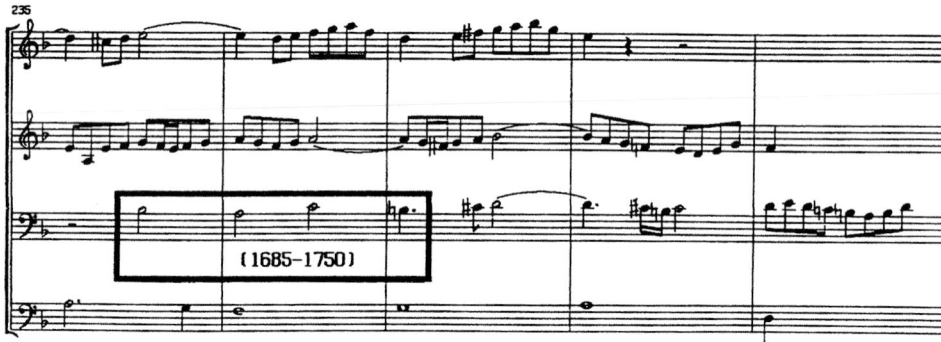

Figure 10.2

Everyday creativity again

Just as J.S. Bach used variation on a theme and repetition to write his last works of music, so we see young children developing the same strategies. It is as if they are biologically and socioculturally driven to do so.

It is interesting to find how often children, as J.S. Bach did, use their own name as an important reference point in their creativity. William (seven years) does this when writing a 'thank you' letter to his grandparents. His creativity is not constrained; he feels able to celebrate the gift he has received, and the joy bubbles through in the handwriting. This is not a commonplace, dutiful piece of writing. It would not score high on punctuation, spelling, letter formation or content, but it went to his grandparents' hearts, which is what a 'thank you' letter should do. It held a creative idea, decorating the letters with spirals, which he was able to develop and make into a creation.

Figure 10.3

William showed a different kind of creativity when he tried his first piece of free writing. The story reflects his love of birds and his fascination with how they fly and how wings work. It shows his assertiveness in marking the end of the story, just to be clear that he doesn't want any adults to suggest he should write more. The story is complete and succinct, and needs no more to be said. It has a visual quality because the letters change size and position in the last sentence as the swallow swoops. It gave him great pleasure to write this story. Again, adults helped him, rather than constraining his creativity, by giving him the personal space to develop his creative idea.

Figure 10.4

The first seven years are the most effective period in cultivating the creativity of children as lifelong learners. Joanna Glover writes that typically:

> Around the age of 6 or 7, children cross a watershed in their musical thinking that brings a new possibility into play in terms of music-making. This is the point at which they become able not just to make, but to think of, musical 'pieces' as such. The realisation comes that the music they create has its own existence, as apart from the activity of making it. The music can be listened to, sung or played by others, captured and kept, and revisited at any time.
>
> (Glover, 2000: 55)

She gives a delightful example of a seven-year-old girl saying she had made a 'composement'. However, Glover stresses that while children come to understand that a musical composition, a dance they choreograph, a story they write or a mathematical pattern they make can be repeated again and again, it is also important to continue to encourage the other side of creativity, which lies in the continuous and lifelong development of its processes. Glover therefore values opportunities which give children time and provision for musical improvisations.

This is a serious point, since, as Pound and Harrison (2002: 139–140) point out, 'Most of the singing in schools and nurseries is of songs that have been written by others.'

Starting school – a vulnerable moment for the development of creativity

In most parts of the world, children do not start their schooling until the age of six or seven years.

Children who have been encouraged to develop deep interests which absorb them and allow them to be separate individuals are also strengthened in their learning to make deep connections and relationships with other people. They put energy into becoming symbol users, with flights of imagination and technical and structural strategies they can bring to bear so that ideas can become creations, when the child wants that.

In this book we have seen that the emergent, early flickerings of creativity are there in babies and toddlers. If we are determined, creativity can be an inclusive part of human development. If these beginnings are cultivated, they begin to develop into increasing possibilities for being a creative thinker who, from time to time, when the situation is conducive, will make creations that may be of the humanities, artistic or scientific.

For many reasons, it is worth cultivating creativity in babies, toddlers and young children. Young children who have learned what it is to be creative and to create are beginning to see that they can deepen the enjoyment, fascination and commitment to learning and living when they have found ways in which to put energy into their creative selves.

Below you will find a summary of the important things that need to be considered in cultivating the creativity of young children.

In this book we have explored the differences and relationship between creative processes and creative products. We have examined how to cultivate creativity:

* Any child has the possibility to develop creativity
* Creativity is found in the arts, sciences and the humanities. It is in all areas of human knowledge and learning
* Crafts and creativity are not the same. Be sure to know the difference, and to value each in different ways
* Performing dances, music, etc. is not the same as creating dances and music. Be sure to know the difference
* Children with disabilities can be creative, too. Creativity embraces diversity and includes everyone
* Creativity does not mean encouraging revolution and chaos in children
* Children are more able to be creative if they feel loved, valued and that they matter. They need to feel emotionally safe
* Creativity is about knowing yourself and valuing your personal space
* Creativity requires children to be autonomous enough to have a sense of control over materials and how they use them
* Children often like to be in the company of others they trust when they create
* Creativity brings into existence new ideas and original ways of doing things
* Creative ideas need to be gathered, and prepared, to incubate, then to hatch
* Adults are important in cultivating a child's creativity
* The quality of the learning environment is of central importance indoors and outdoors in encouraging creativity
* The process of creativity is as important as the product
* The creations children make are very personal, and children may not want to share them widely
* Children need the right help at the right time in the right way
* Children need to be helped to develop the technical know-how necessary in order to be creative
* Most creativity is of the everyday kind. Some people become specialists in a particular kind of creativity. Some make world-shattering creations that change the world
* The first seven years are a crucial time in cultivating a child's creativity.

Reflective questions

Take a look at the environment indoors and out of doors in your setting. How does it encourage creativity? How do you support the processes of creativity? How do you show the children you value their creations? How much time and energy do you devote to developing your own creativity, so that you live as fulfilled a life as possible, remembering that creativity is about feeling fully alive?

Make an action plan. Identify two things you will do to support the processes and two things to support the creations of children, using what you have learned from reading the book and reflecting on your practice.

Useful texts

Davies, M. (2003) *Movement and Dance in Early Childhood, 2nd Edition.* Paul Chapman Publishing: London.

Frohlich, C. (2009) Chapter 22, Vitality in music and dance as basic existential experience: Applications in teaching music, in S. Malloch and C. Trevarthen (eds) *Communicative Musicality: Exploring the Basis of Human Companionship.* Oxford University Press: Oxford

Matthews, J. (2003) *Drawing and Painting: Children and Visual Representation, 2nd Edition.* Paul Chapman Publishing: London.

Bibliography

Abbott, L. and Moyles, H. (1999) *Early Education Transformed*. Falmer Press: London.

Athey, C. (1990) *Extending Learning: A Parent/Teacher Partnership*. Paul Chapman Publishing: London.

Bartholomew, L. and Bruce, T. (1993) *Getting to Know You: A Guide to Record Keeping in Early Childhood Education and Care*. Paul Chapman Publishing: London.

Bettelheim, B. (1977) *The Uses of Enchantment*. Vintage Books: New York.

Blakemore, S.J. (2000) Early Years Learning. *Parliamentary Office of Science and Technology Report 140*, pp. 1–12.

Bruce, T. (1991) *Time to Play in Early Childhood Education and Care.* Hodder Arnold: London.

Bruce, T. (2004) *Developing Learning in Early Childhood.* Paul Chapman Publishing: London.

Bruce, T. (2011a) *Learning Through Play: Babies, Toddlers and the Foundation Years, 2nd Edition.* Hodder Education: London.

Bruce, T. (2011b) *Early Childhood Education, 4th Edition*. Hodder Education: London.

Bruce, T., Meggitt, C. and Grenier, J. (2010) *Child Care and Education, 5th Edition.* Hodder Education: London.

Bruce, T. and Spratt, J. (2011) *Essentials of Literacy from 0–7: A Whole-child Approach to Communication. Language and Literacy.* Sage: London.

Bunting, J. (2003) *Learning Through Sustained Imaginative Play at Tachbrook Nursery School.* Centre for Literacy in Primary Education (CLPE) for the City of Westminster.

Burgers, W. and Verbraakt, C.A. (1957) A new approach to the problem of the origin of the cube-texture Rowland Transformation. *Acta Metallurgica,* Vol. 5, No. 12, pp. 765–767.

Carr, M. (1999) Being a learner: Five dispositions for early childhood. *Early Childhood Practice: The Journal for Multi-Professional Partnerships,* Vol. 1, No. 1, pp. 81–100.

Carter, R. (1998) *Mapping the Mind*. Seven Dials: London.

Christiansen, A. (2002) Play, imagination and communication: Analyses of mobile phone play. *Early Childhood Practice: The Journal for Multi-Professional Partnerships,* Vol. 4, No. 2, pp. 50–61.

Corsaro, W. (1979) 'We're friends, right?' Children's use of access rituals in a nursery school. *Language in Society,* Vol. 8, pp. 315–316.

Craft, A. (2002) *Creativity and Early Years Education: A Lifewide Foundation.* Continuum: London and New York.

Damasio, A. (1999) *The Feeling of What Happens: Body and Emotion in the Making of Consciousness.* Heinemann: London.

Davies, M. (2003) *Movement and Dance in Early Childhood, 2nd Edition.* Paul Chapman Publishing: London.

Dixon, P. (2003) *Weepers: A Collection of Poems Lamenting the Disgraces of the National Curriculum in Primary and Nursery Education.* 30 Cheriton Road, Winchester, Hants.

Donaldson, M. (1992) *Human Minds: An Exploration.* Allen Lane, The Penguin Press: London.

Duffy, B. (2009) *Supporting Creativity and Imagination in the Early Years, 2nd Edition.* Open University Press: Maidenhead, Philadelphia.

Duncan, I. (1930) *My Life.* Victor Gollancz: London.

Dunkin, D. and Hanna, P. (2001) *Thinking Together: Quality Adult/Child Interactions.* New Zealand Council for Educational Research: Wellington, NZ.

Edmunds, F. (1979) *Rudolf Steiner Education: The Waldorf Schools.* Rudolf Steiner Press: London.

Elkington, J. (2001) *The Chrysalis Economy: How Citizens, CEOs and Corporations Can Fuse Values and Value Creation.* Capstone: Oxford.

Etheridge, K. (2001) All That Remains: Parts 1 and 2. A mixed media installation. *Early Childhood Practice: The Journal for Multi-Professional Partnerships.* Vol. 3, No. 2, pp. 7–9.

Fabius, C. (1998) *Mehndi: The Art of Henna Body Painting.* Three Rivers Press: New York.

Forbes, R. (2004) *Beginning to Play from Birth to Three.* Open University Press: Maidenhead, Philadelphia.

Glover, J. (2000) *Children Composing 4–14.* Routledge Falmer: London.

Goddard–Blythe, S. (2004) First steps to the most important ABC. *Times Educational Supplement,* 7 January, p. 23.

Gopnik, A., Meltzoff, A. and Kuhl, P. (1999) *How Babies Think.* Weidenfeld and Nicolson: London.

Goswami, U. (1998) *Cognition in Children.* Psychology Press: Hove.

Gregg, E. (1968) *What To Do When There Is Nothing To Do: A Mother's Handbook – 601 Tested Play Ideas for Young Children.* Dell Publishing Co.: New York.

Gura, P. (ed.) (1992) directed by Tina Bruce with the Froebel Blockplay Research Group, *Exploring Learning: Young Children and Blockplay.* Paul Chapman Publishing: London.

Gura, P. (1996) *Resources for Early Learning: Children, Adults and Stuff.* Paul Chapman Publishing: London.

Gussin Paley, V. (1984) *Boys and Girls: Superheroes in the Doll Corner.* Chicago University Press: Chicago.

Harris, P. (2000) *The Work of the Imagination.* Blackwell Publishers: Oxford.

Hewitt, P. (2002) Chief Executive, Arts Council of England, Extracts from his speech: Beyond Boundaries. *Early Childhood Practice: The Journal for Multi-Professional Practice,* Vol. 4, No. 2, pp. 25–29.

Hofstadter, D. (2000) *Godel, Escher, Bach: An Eternal Golden Braid.* Penguin Books: London.

Holland, P. (2003) *We Don't Play with Guns Here: War, Weapons and Superhero Play in the Early Years.* Open University Press: London, Maidenhead, Philadelphia.

Howkins, J. (2001) *The Creative Economy: How People Make Money from Ideas.* Allen Lane, The Penguin Press: London.

Hyder, T. (2004) *War, Conflict and Play.* Open University Press: Maidenhead, Philadelphia.

Jansson, T. (2003) *The Summer Book.* Sort of Books, Penguin Group: London.

Kalliala, M. (2005) *Play Culture in a Changing World.* Open University Press, McGraw-Hill: Maidenhead.

Karmiloff-Smith, A. (1992) *Beyond Modularity: A Developmental Perspective on Cognitive Science.* A Bradford Book, MIT: Cambridge, MA and London.

Keynes, R. (2002) *Annie's Box.* Fourth Estate: London.

Kitzinger, C. (1997) Born to be good? What motivates us to be good, bad or indifferent towards others? *New Internationalist,* April, pp. 15–17.

Koestler, A. (1964) *The Act of Creation.* Picador, Pan Books: London.

Laevers, F. (ed.) (1994) *The Innovative Project, 'Experiential Education' and the Definition of Quality in Education.* Katholieke Universiteit: Leuven.

Langer, E. (1997) *The Power of Mindful Learning.* Addison/Wesley Publishing Company: Harlow.

Liebschner, J. (1992) *A Child's Work: Freedom and Guidance in Froebel's Educational Theory and Practice.* Lutterworth: Cambridge.

Lively, P. (1993) *Cleopatra's Sister.* Penguin Books: Harmondsworth.

Longhorn, F. (1988) *A Sensory Curriculum for Very Special People: A Practical Approach to Curriculum Planning.* Condor Books, Souvenir Press (E and A) Ltd: London.

Mandela, N. (1993) Acceptance Speech of the President of the African National Congress, at the Nobel Peace Prize Award Ceremony, Oslo, Norway, 10 December, www.anc.org.za

Manning-Morton, J. and Thorp, M. (2003) *Key Times for Play.* Open University Press: Maidenhead, Philadelphia.

Marshall, S. (1963) *An Experiment in Education.* Cambridge University Press: Cambridge.

Maslow, A. (1973) *The Farther Reaches of Human Nature.* Penguin: Harmondsworth.

Matterson, E. (1975) *Play with a Purpose for Under Sevens, 2nd Edition.* Penguin: Harmondsworth.

Matthews, J. (2003) *Drawing and Painting: Children and Visual Representation, 2nd Edition.* Paul Chapman Publishing: London.

McKellar, P. (1957) *Imagination and Thinking.* Cohen and West: London.

Malloch, S. and Trevarthen, C. (eds) (2009) *Communicative Musicality: Exploring the Basis of Human Companionship.* Oxford University Press: Oxford.

Murray, L. and Andrews, E. (2000) *The Social Baby.* CP Publishing: Richmond, Surrey.

Nielsen, L. (1992) *Space and Self: Active Learning by Means of the Little Room.* Sikon Press: Copenhagen, Denmark. (Available from RNIB Education.)

Niethammer, C. (1977) *Daughters of the Earth: The Lives and Legends of American Indian Women.* Collier Books, Macmillan Publishing Company: London and New York.

Ockelford, A. (2008) *Music for Children and Young People with Complex Needs.* Oxford University Press: Oxford.

Orr, R. (2003) *My Right to Play: A Child with Complex Needs.* Open University Press: Maidenhead, Philadelphia.

Ouvry, M. (2004) *Sounds Like Play.* Early Education: London.

Papert, S. (1980) *Mind Storms: Children, Computers and Powerful Ideas.* Harvester Press: Brighton.

Piaget, J. (1947) *The Psychology of Intelligence.* Translated by M. Piercy and D. Berlyne. Routledge and Kegan Paul: London.

Piaget, J. (1952) *Play, Dreams and Imitation.* Translated by C. Gattegno and F. Hodgson. Routledge and Kegan Paul: London.

Pound, L. and Harrison, C. (2002) *Supporting Musical Development in the Early Years.* Open University Press: Maidenhead, Philadelphia.

Pullman, P. (2002) A National Curriculum worth having. *Times Educational Supplement,* 8 February.

RNIB (1995) *Play it My Way: Learning Through Play with Your Visually Impaired Child.* HMSO: London.

Rowland, P. (1954–1955) A three-dimensional face-centred cubic model for the study of crystal phenomena. *Journal of the Institute of Metals,* Vol. 83, pp. 455–495.

Steiner, R. (1988) *The Child's Changing Consciousness and Waldorf Education.* Rudolf Steiner Press: London.

Storr, A. (1989) *Solitude.* HarperCollins: London.

Te Whariki (1996) *Early Childhood Curriculum.* New Zealand Ministry of Education. Learning Media: Wellington.

Tovey, H. (2007) *Playing Outdoors: Spaces and Places, Risk and Challenge.* Open University Books: Maidenhead.

Trevarthen, C. (1998) The child's need to learn a culture, in M. Woodhead, D. Faulkner and K. Littleton, *Cultural Worlds of Early Childhood.* Routledge in association with Open University Press: London and New York.

Vila, I. (1996) Intentionality, communication and language, in A. Tryphon and J. Voneche (eds) *Piaget–Vygotsky: The Social Genesis of Thought.* Psychology Press: Hove.

Vygotsky, L. (1978) *Mind in Society.* Harvard University Press: London and Cambridge, MA.

Winnicott, D. (1971) *Playing and Reality.* Penguin: Harmondsworth.

Winnicott, D. (1990) The capacity to be alone. In D. Winnicott, *The Maturational Processes and the Facilitating Environment: Studies in the Theory of Emotional Development.* Karnac Books: London.

Index